Within each of us is a dream—a heart's desire.

For some, it's a professional or career goal; for others, it's a relationship or a family. It might be a political or social desire, or it may be a religious or spiritual one.

Unfortunately, many people are not pursuing their heart's desire. Some are so far away from living their dream that they have forgotten what their dream truly is.

The good news is that with every dream comes the time and the ability to fulfill it. The bad news? Many people use that time and ability *doing something else*—something that often has little or nothing to do with their dream.

Why? What's keeping us from fulfilling our heart's desire? Why aren't we living our dreams?

Our comfort zone.

Our comfort zone includes all the things we've done often enough to feel comfortable doing. Any behavior outside our comfort zone can result in fear, guilt, unworthiness, hurt feelings, anger, discouragement—you know: discomfort.

Alas, to accomplish something new requires new behavior, and new behavior by its very definition lies outside the confines of the comfort zone.

So, do we honor our comfort zone, or do we honor our dream? The choice is ours.

As John Kenneth Galbraith pointed out, "When faced with the choice between changing and proving there's no need to do so, most people get busy on the proof."

DO IT! is a book for those

- who want to discover—clearly and precisely—their dream;

- who choose to pursue that dream, even if it means learning (and—gasp!—practicing) some new behavior;

- who wouldn't mind having some fun along the way; and

- who are willing to expand their comfort zone enough to include their heart's desire—and maybe even a dance floor.

The secret lies in the doing. As Woody Allen said, "Eighty percent of success is showing up." And J. Paul Getty agreed: "Rise early. Work late. Strike oil."

PRELUDE:
What If?

What if you were a Master Creator?

What if you were so good at creating, you could create anything you wanted from seemingly nothing at all?

What if you were so good at creation that you were famous for it? (In the Olympics of Creation, you were a multi-Gold Medalist.)

What if you were so good at creation, creation started becoming dull? Although you had the admiration of world after world (some of which you helped create), you began to miss the challenge you felt earlier in your creative career.

What if you had a chance to relive "the thrill of victory and the agony of defeat" you so enjoyed at some former time and place?

So, Master Creator that you are, you created a button marked "Greater Challenge."

You considered all that might be contained in the concept of "Greater Challenge," decided Greater Challenge would probably provide some of the excitement and satisfaction you missed from your apprentice days, took a deep breath, pushed the button...

...and found yourself where you are right now—feeling what you're feeling now, thinking what you're thinking now, with everything in your life precisely the way it is now—reading this book.

Men are born to succeed,
not to fail.

HENRY DAVID THOREAU

DO IT!
Let's Get Off Our Buts

by

John-Roger and Peter McWilliams

ISBN 0-931580-96-X

Book and Cover Design: Paul LeBus

Editorial Consultants: Zachery Cook, Annika Cropper,
Joy S. Lindsley, Victoria Marine, Mark Penzer,
Pat O'Hara, Patti Rayner, Jean Sedillos, Heide Smith,
Bernice Stangrover, Annette Wylie

Photography: Betty Bennett

Desktop Publishing: Sara J. Thomas

If your local bookstore is out, you may order additional
copies by calling

1-800-LIFE-101

Prelude Press

8159 Santa Monica Boulevard, Los Angeles, California 90046

Regret for the things we did
can be tempered by time;
it is regret for the things we
did not do that is inconsolable.

SYDNEY J. HARRIS

CONTENTS

PART TWO
BUILT FOR SUCCESS 77

PART THREE
DISCOVERING AND CHOOSING OUR DREAMS 133

PART FOUR
BECOMING PASSIONATE

PART FIVE
DOING IT

PART SIX
LIVING YOUR DREAMS

I might repeat to myself,
slowly and soothingly,
a list of quotations beautiful
from minds profound—
if I can remember
any of the damn things.

DOROTHY PARKER

*Properly, we should
read for power.
Man reading
should be
man intensely alive.
The book should be
a ball of light
in one's hand.*

EZRA POUND

INTRODUCTION: How Do You Do?

We all have a dream, a heart's desire. Most have more than one. Some of us have an entire entourage. This is a book about discovering (or rediscovering) those dreams, how to choose which dreams to pursue, and practical suggestions for achieving them.

There's a lot of good news about our dreams:

- By pursuing any *one* of our dreams, we can find fulfillment. We don't need to pursue them all.

- We don't have to *achieve* a dream in order to find fulfillment—we need only actively *pursue* the dream to attain satisfaction.

- By living our dream, we can contribute not only to ourselves, but to everyone and everything around us.

And yet, with all this good news, most people are not pursuing their dreams.

When we're not pursuing our dreams, we spend our time and abilities pursuing the things we *think* will make us happy, the things we *believe* will bring us fulfillment: the new house, the new car, the new cashmere jump suit.

There's an old saying: "You can't get enough of what you don't really want." When the new car doesn't make us happy, we tend to blame the new car for not being "enough," and set our sights on a "better" new car. Surely *that* will make us happy.

Many people are so far away from living their dream that *they have forgotten what their dream truly is.*

It is sad. It is unnecessary. It is wasteful. And yet, it's so common an ailment that it's become a cliché. We have abandoned our heart's desire—and somewhere, deep down, we know it. Even if we don't remember quite what it is—we miss it.

The three stages of a man's life:
1. He believes in Santa Claus.
2. He doesn't believe in Santa Claus.
3. He is Santa Claus.

I stopped believing in Santa Claus
when my mother took me to
see him in a department store,
and he asked for my autograph.

SHIRLEY TEMPLE

Why aren't we living our dreams?

Because there is something we are trained to honor more than our dreams: the comfort zone.

The comfort zone is all the things we have done often enough to feel comfortable doing again. Whenever we do something new, it falls outside the barrier of the comfort zone. In even *contemplating* a new action, we feel fear, guilt, unworthiness, hurt feelings, anger—all those things we generally think of as "uncomfortable."

When we feel uncomfortable enough long enough, we tend to feel discouraged (a form of exhaustion), and we return to thoughts, feelings and actions that are more familiar, more practiced, more predictable—more, well, comfortable.

The irony is that the feelings we have been taught to label "uncomfortable" are, in fact, among the very tools necessary to fulfill our dreams. As it turns out, the bricks used to build the walls of comfort zone are made of gold.

Why don't we know this?

The training we received as children—which, for the most part, is appropriate for children—is not appropriate for adults. The rules of an independent, productive adult are not the same rules of a dependent, limited child. What is true for children can be counterproductive for adults. We live our lives as though it were a bicycle with the training wheels still in place—limiting, entirely *too* safe, and somewhat boring.

We no longer believe in Santa Claus, but we still believe that "being uncomfortable" is reason enough not to do something new. The Easter Bunny hopped out of our lives years ago, yet we still let "what other people might think" affect our behavior. The tooth fairy was yanked from our consciousness long before adolescence, but we still feel we can justify any personal failure by finding someone or something outside ourselves to blame.

*There are some people
that if they don't know,
you can't tell 'em.*

LOUIS ARMSTRONG

Most people are drifting along in a childish sleep. To live our dreams, we must wake up.

In reading that last sentence, do you feel your comfort zone being challenged? That will happen a lot in this book. That tingling we feel when we contemplate waking up and living our dreams we can label either "fear" or "excitement." No matter what we call it, it's the same feeling. If we call it fear, it's an uncomfortable feeling, and we tend to find reasons not to read any further. If we call it excitement, we turn it into energy that makes the process of learning and doing an active, enjoyable one.

It's your choice. It's always your choice. The trouble is, many of us have delegated that choice to habits formed long ago, formed when we knew far less about life than we know now. We let habits formed when we were two or four or six or ten or fifteen control our lives today.

To change a habit requires work. Make no mistake about it: reading this book will not change your life, just as reading a guidebook to France will not show you France. It may give you a *sense* of France, perhaps, but France is France and can only be experienced through *action*.

And so it is with your dreams. This book will show you *how* to discover your dreams, *how* to select the dreams you choose to pursue, and *how* to fulfill those dreams— but if you don't *act* upon those *how's,* you will never see Paris from atop the Eiffel Tower.

Although fulfilling our dreams requires *work,* the process can also be *fun.* Which reminds us of a joke.

An Indian Chief greeted a friend by raising his hand in the traditional salute and saying, "Chance!"

"Chance?" his friend asked, "You must mean 'How!'"

"I know how," the Chief responded, "I'm looking for chance."

This book is your chance. It's a chance *you* are giving *yourself.* Imagine for a moment that you are powerful enough to have had this book written *just for you.* When

*If you're not playing
a big enough game,
you'll screw up
the game you're playing
just to give yourself
something to do.*

you get a sense of that power, you'll know that you have all it takes to fulfill your dream. *Any* dream. *Your* dream.

F. Scott Fitzgerald met Joan Crawford at a Hollywood party. He told her that he had been hired to write the screenplay for her next film. She looked him straight in the eye and said, "Write hard, Mr. Fitzgerald, write hard."

Imagine that we co-authors are looking you straight in the eye and saying, "Dream big, dear reader, dream big."

What's *our* Big Dream? Well, we call the 1990's *The DO IT! Decade*. It's not just ten years at the end of a century, but the culmination of an entire *millennium*. For a thousand years, the collective hearts of humanity have had some worthwhile dreams—world peace, harmony with one's self and neighbors, an environment in which all things can grow and prosper, a respect for all life.

Well, we think it's time to DO IT!

This global fulfillment doesn't demand the *sacrifice* of personal dreams. It merely requires the *alignment* of personal dreams to a larger vision.

When we discover how easy it is to fulfill personal dreams—even the ones that seem "really big" before the achievement of them—we are naturally inspired to fulfill even larger dreams: our global, universal dreams.

The truth is, pursuing a Big Dream of our own choosing is the same amount of work as gathering more and more of the things you don't really want. You're going to spend the rest of your life doing *something*. It might as well be something *you* want to do.

"But what about money? But what about time? But what about this? But what about that?" We'll get to all that (and all this, too). There are a lot of *buts* to "get off" before we can even *consider* living our dreams.

Let's bring this Introduction to a close by answering the question we posed at the beginning: "How do you do?"

That's easy. You do by learning.

"Great. And how do you learn?"

*Do not be too timid
and squeamish
about your actions.
All life is an experiment.*

RALPH WALDO EMERSON

You learn by doing.

A chicken-and-egg conundrum, to be sure; yet one that can easily be penetrated by this deceptively simple thought: "The willingness to do creates the ability to do."

For now, simply be *willing* to do. Be willing to do what it takes to read this book. That takes the willingness to finish this page and turn to the next. That takes the willingness to finish this paragraph. That takes the willingness to finish this sentence (which you have just done—congratulations!).

Where does the willingness come from?

From you.

As Joni Mitchell pointed out, "It all comes down to you."

We certainly agree, and would only add, "It all comes down to *do*."

☆

This book is part of *The LIFE 101 Series*. The series includes the umbrella (overview) book *LIFE 101: Everything We Wish We Had Learned About Life In School—But Didn't,* as well as *You Can't Afford the Luxury of a Negative Thought: A Book for People with Any Life-Threatening Illness—Including Life.* Although all the books in the series support each other, each stands independently and can be read separately.

"Let's Go."
"Yes, let's go."
Stage Direction:
They do not move.

LAST LINES OF *WAITING FOR GODOT*
SAMUEL BECKETT

PART ONE

WHY WE'RE NOT
LIVING OUR DREAMS

You may find this first part of the book depressing. We're going to explain why most people aren't living their dreams—and we're not going to pull any punches.

It's not a pretty picture.

We want to make it clear that the reason we aren't living our dreams is *inside ourselves*. For the most part, however, we *pretend* it's people, things and situations *outside ourselves* that are to blame. (Not enough money, education, contacts, intelligence, looks, etc., etc.)

If you find it depressing to take a detailed look at the trap in which many people find themselves, take heart—there are five more sections, each more optimistic than the last.

On the other hand, you might find this an uplifting section. You may say, on more than one occasion, "So *that's* why that happens!" Knowing the truth about the cause of something—especially after so many years of being misled—can be liberating.

Further, when we know that the *cause* of something is in ourselves, and that we (ourselves) are one of the few things in this universe that we have the right and the ability to change, we begin to get a sense of the choices we really do have, an inkling of the power we have, a feeling of being in charge—of our lives, of our future, of our dreams.

Pithy quote to come.

This Was Going to Be a Truly Great Opening Chapter, But...

This was going to be the best opening chapter you could possibly imagine, but so many things got in the way.

We were going to spend lots of time writing it, but, well, you know how time goes!

We were going to get lots of touching and poignant and humorous examples of people not getting things done, but we never got around to interviewing the people.

We were going to gather lots of wonderful quotes to illustrate our points, but we left the quote book at home, and this chapter is being written at a lecture hall outside Carmel, California. (Besides, we think the dog ate it.)

We were going to make sure that this chapter was so informative, so readable and so wonderful that if you were reading it in a bookstore, you'd buy the book, or, if you were reading it in a library, you'd check it out, or, if you were reading it at home, you'd decide, "Boy, I'm certainly going to enjoy reading *this* book!" but we decided to watch this movie on TV last night, and we were going to work on the chapter afterward, but then we went out for ice cream, and then we were tired, and decided to start fresh in the morning, but then we slept late, and then we went out for breakfast and took a drive past an aquarium and decided to stop in, then we went for lunch, and then thought we'd take a nap and start fresh in the evening, but then we started watching a documentary on TV, then, of course, it was time for dinner, then we were invited to the movies, and we don't want to be rude to our friends, and besides we sort-of wanted to see the movie anyway, then we were going to go right back and work on this chapter, but then we remembered how good the ice cream was the night before...

Do or do not.
There is no try.

YODA

But

But—that three-letter, four-letter word. It permeates our language. It's a nasty little word. It allows us to lie to ourselves—and to severely limit ourselves—without even knowing it.

Let's look at a typical sentence containing "but."

"I want to visit my sick grandmother, but it's too cold outside."

When used in that kind of sentence, "but" usually means: "Ignore all that good-sounding stuff that went before—here comes the truth." We might even consider BUT an acronym for Behold the Underlying Truth. (And BUTS can be shortened to BS.)

The truth within the above sentence is that grandma is not getting a visit. The lie is that we *care* so much about our sick grandmother that we *really want to* pay her a visit. (Note our *sensitivity* to her need for visitation, and our *compassion* for wanting to visit her.)

At this point, entering stage right, are two of *but's* dearest friends—*if only* and *try*.

"*If only* it were a fine spring day, I'd be into the woods and on my way to Grandmother's house. *If only* it weren't so darn *cold*, I'd be at Granny's side right now. I'm going to *try* to get there tomorrow!"

Unless, of course, we are too busy, too poor, too tired, too _____ (please fill in the blank with one of your favorites), or perhaps not feeling all that good ourselves.

But even if we and everything else were fine and dandy, let's not forget the about the *wolves*...

*Success is simply
a matter of luck.
Ask any failure.*

EARL WILSON

Yes-But

The naked "but" is what we use when ignoring our own good advice. When ignoring the unbearably good advice from another source, we use the hyphenated version: "yes-but."

In a sentence, it might seem as though these were two words—separated by a period, or at least a coma. They are, in fact, a hyphenate: yes-but. There would be no "yes" if the "but" were not close behind—and attached.

"You really should pay your car insurance."

"Yes-but, I don't get paid until next week."

"You could get a cash advance on your credit card."

"Yes-but, I owe so much already."

"If you have an accident you'll have no insurance."

"Yes-but, I'll drive real careful."

And on and on.

When we argue for our limitations, we get to keep them. *Yes-but* means, "Here come the arguments for my limitations." Or, if you favor acronyms, YES-BUT = "Your Evaluation is Superb—Behold the Underlying Truth."

The only thing more foolish than a person pouring forth a stream of "yes-buts" is the person who continues to give good advice in the face of obvious indifference.

"Yes-but, I thought if I tried *just once more,* it might be the bit of wisdom that would *change their lives.*"

Uh huh. And what did Jesus have to say about this? "Give not which is holy unto the dogs, neither cast ye your pearls before swine, lest they trample them under their feet, and turn again and rend you." (Matthew 7,6)*

"Ouch."

---

*Those who study the Bible and would like to know the Scriptural reference for much of this book, please read Matthew, chapter 7.

Results! Why, man,
I have gotten a lot of results.
I know several thousand
things that won't work.

THOMAS A. EDISON

Reasons or Results

In any given area of life, we have one of two things: reasons or results—excuses or experiences, stories or successes, justifications or justice.

We either have what we want, or we have ironclad, airtight, impenetrable reasons why it was not even *marginally possible* to get it.

We use one of the most powerful tools *at* our disposal—the mind—*for* our disposal. Rather than dispose of the barriers to our dreams, the mind disposes of the dreams.

In the amount of time it takes for the mind to invent a good excuse, it could have created an alternate way of achieving the desired result—rendering excuse-making unnecessary.

But, alas, as John Kenneth Galbraith pointed out, "In the choice between changing one's mind and proving there's no need to do so, most people get busy on the proof."

While we're on the subject of the mind, let's give the mind something to ponder—a premise we'll be considering throughout the book...

It is hard to fight an enemy
who has outposts in your head.

SALLY KEMPTON

We Live the Life We Choose

Here's the premise: We are all, right now, living the life of our own choosing.

This choice, of course, is not a single, monumental choice. No one decides, for example, "I'm going to move to LA, and in five years I want to be a waiter in a so-so restaurant, planning to get my pictures done real soon now so that I can find an agent and become a star," or, "I'm going to marry a dreadful person and we'll live together in a loveless marriage, staying together only for the kids, who I don't really like, either."

No. The choices we're talking about here are made daily, hourly, moment by moment.

Do we try something new, or stick to the tried-and-true? Do we take a risk, or eat what's already on our dish? (No more of these will rhyme—honest.) Do we ponder a thrilling adventure, or contemplate what's on TV? Do we walk over and meet that interesting stranger, or do we play it safe? Do we indulge our heart, or cater to our fear?

The bottom-line question: Do we pursue what we want, or do we do what's comfortable?

For the most part, most people most often choose comfort—the familiar, the time-honored, the well-worn but well-known. After a lifetime of choosing between comfort and risk, we are left with the life we currently have.

And it was all of our own choosing.

*The only thing I can't stand
is discomfort.*

GLORIA STEINEM

The Comfort Zone

The comfort zone is our personal area of thoughts and actions within which we feel comfortable; it's all the things we've done (or thought) often enough to feel comfortable doing (or thinking). Anything we haven't done (or thought) often enough to feel comfortable doing lies outside the parameters of the comfort zone. When we do (or think) these things (basically, anything new) we feel uncomfortable.*

For example, most people reading this book find little difficulty reading English—it's within their comfort zone. But how comfortable are you reading code? Here's a sentence in code:

Dpohsbuvmbujpot! Zpv'wf kvtu dsbdlfe uif dpef!

Can you crack the code? Each of the letters stands for another letter in the alphabet. They are arranged in a logical way so that when you know the code, you'll be able to decipher the sentence. What does the sentence say?

How do you feel? Uncomfortable? Overwhelmed? Have you given up? Did you give up before even starting? What if we told you there was $100,000 riding on solving the puzzle? In addition to *money*, what if you had to solve it *on television?* And, in addition to that, what if there was a *time limit* imposed? Say, three minutes. What if something *really bad* were to happen to someone you love if you couldn't crack the code in three minutes? What if he or she were *really counting on you?*

How do you feel? If you played along with our questions, you probably felt some tinges of fear, guilt, unworthiness, hurt feelings and/or anger—the feelings we lump into the general category of *uncomfortable*.

---

*For the purposes of simplicity, while talking about the comfort zone, when we mention "actions," assume we've included "thoughts," too. It will save cluttering up the next few chapters with several hundred "(or thoughts)."

*We act as though comfort and
luxury were the chief
requirements of life,
when all that we need
to make us happy
is something
to be enthusiastic about.*

CHARLES KINGSLEY

After feeling uncomfortable enough long enough, we tend to feel discouraged; we give up. Some people gave up before they even began. They were permanently discouraged about word puzzles. They told themselves, "I'm no good at this sort of thing," and skipped to the next paragraph. Unfortunately, there we were in the next paragraph—waiting for them—reminding them of the puzzle—making them feel uncomfortable. (More on who *really* makes who feel uncomfortable later.)

Other people, who love puzzles, jumped right in. They weren't uncomfortable; they were *challenged*. They hung in there, and some of them solved it (and are now wondering how they can collect their $100,000 prize). Perhaps the "doers" felt the same emotion the uncomfortable felt—that tingling we feel when rising to a challenge—and labeled it "excitement" instead of "fear." Maybe they *used* that energy to help solve the puzzle.

OK. Try again. This time we'll give you a clue: The first letter is a C.

Dpohsbuvmbujpot! Zpv'wf kvtu dsbdlfe uif dpef!

Compare the relationship between C and the first letter of the puzzle (D) and see if you can see a pattern. If you see one, try it on the next several letters and see if something approaching a word emerges. If not, look for another pattern.

Some people are now actively involved in the process of figuring it out. Others are still saying, "I can't do these things." As Henry Ford said, "If you think you can do a thing or think you can't do a thing, you're right." If we say we can't do something, we don't spend any time on it, therefore we can't. A self-fulfilling prophecy.

So, if you're still in the "can't" category, switch it around. Tell yourself, out loud, "I *can* solve this," and become involved. Invest a little *time* in the process. "The willingness to do creates the ability to do." Give yourself the willingness. (A pencil might help, too.)

You have to leave
the city of your comfort
and go into the wilderness
of your intuition.
What you'll discover
will be wonderful.
What you'll discover
will be yourself.

ALAN ALDA

What is the relationship between C and D? Where have you seen them together before? Where are they *always* together, one right after the other?

Dpohsbuvmbujpot! Zpv'wf kvtu dsbdlfe uif dpef!

Another clue? ("I'd like to buy a vowel, please.") The second letter is O. What's the relationship between O and P? It's the same relationship as between C and D. ("Living together, no children.")

Most people have, of course, figured it out by now. (There. Does *that* make you feel uncomfortable? Those who haven't figured it out don't like to think they're *behind* most people, and those who have figured it out don't like to be thought of as "most people.")

Our final clue: the alphabet. For those of you who don't have your dictionary handy, the alphabet looks like this:

ABCDEFGHIJKLMNOPQRSTUVWXYZ

Now, can you see the relationship between C and D and between O and P? Apply that to the other letters of the puzzle and see what you get. Congratulations! You've just cracked the code!

You'll note that when you move *past* your comfort zone you find adventure, excitement, satisfaction and the answer to some questions you may never have known to ask before. (Although this chapter was more like *Wheel of Fortune*, life is also like *Jeopardy*—you're given the answers; it's often just a matter of asking the right questions. We'll be asking some of those questions in Part Three.)

How often have you heard someone say, "I don't want to do that; I feel uncomfortable."? It is a *given*—for most people an *accepted fact*—*that uncomfortableness is a sufficient reason for not doing something.*

The primary sensations we encounter when approaching the "walls" of the comfort zone are fear, guilt, unworthiness, hurt feelings and anger. When feeling any one—or, especially, a combination of them—we say we're uncomfortable. After tilting the windmills of our comfort zone for

How to Behave in an Elevator

1. *Face forward.*
2. *Fold hands in front.*
3. *Do not make eye contact.*
4. *Watch the numbers.*
5. *Don't talk to anyone you*
   don't know.
6. *Stop talking with anyone*
   you do know when anyone you
   don't know enters the elevator.
7. *Avoid brushing bodies.*

LAYNE LONGFELLOW

a time, we tend to feel discouraged—and discouragement is the primary barrier to living our dreams.

Let's take a closer look at fear, guilt, unworthiness, hurt feelings, anger and discouragement. (Just what you wanted, huh?)

The thing I fear most is fear.

MICHEL EYQUEM DE MONTAIGNE
1580

Nothing is terrible except fear itself.

FRANCIS BACON
1623

The only thing I am afraid of is fear.

DUKE OF WELLINGTON
("THE IRON DUKE")
1831

Nothing is so much to be feared as fear.

HENRY DAVID THOREAU
1841

Fear

We all know what fear feels like. It is probably the most common limiting emotion—and, for many people, the most common emotion, *period*. As Shakespeare pointed out, we are often "distilled almost to jelly with the act of fear."

Not only do we fear new things, we also feel fear *in addition to* other negative emotions. We feel guilt, *and we're afraid to feel the guilt*. We feel pain, *and we're afraid to feel the pain*. Even when we feel fear, we're often afraid to feel the fear. (That's known as "worrying about your worries," "an anxiety attack," or "the screaming meemies.") Shakespeare, again: "Of all base passions, fear is the most accursed."

Because it's so common, fear has many other names: apprehension, misgiving, trepidation, dread, horror, phobia, terror, alarm, consternation, foreboding, qualm, suspicion, fret, uneasiness, distress, panic, etc., etc.

Physically, we feel fear in the area we generally call the stomach. Although it's lower than the physical stomach (more in the area of the lower abdomen), for the sake of locating fear—and going along with the popular use of the word—we'll define "the stomach" as a large, circular area with the navel at its center.

In its more intense forms, the feeling of fear is accompanied by a quickening of the pulse, a widening of the eyes, and a sharpening of the senses.

Someone once described FEAR in an acronym: False Expectations Appearing Real. For the most part, what we fear is not real—it is merely our mind *imagining* something awful that has not yet happened. ("Fear is pain arising from the anticipation of evil," Aristotle said.)

Seldom do we do the thing we fear, so we never discover if our projection of disaster was accurate. In fact, when we *don't* do the thing we are afraid of, we breathe a

*Fear is the main
source of superstition,
and one of the main
sources of cruelty.
To conquer fear is the
beginning of wisdom.*

BERTRAND RUSSELL

*Our greatest pretenses are built up
not to hide the evil and the ugly in us,
but our emptiness. The hardest thing to
hide is something that is not there.*

ERIC HOFFER

sigh of relief *as though it actually would have taken place.* "That was a close one!" we say, even though we never actually got close to anything but a string of our own negative thoughts.

Fear breeds lack of experience, lack of experience breeds ignorance, ignorance breeds more fear. It is a vicious circle.

As Lucretius described it more than two centuries ago, "For as children tremble and fear everything in the blind darkness, so we in the light sometimes fear what is no more to be feared than the things children in the dark hold in terror and imagine will come true."

Put another way, fear is interest paid on a debt you may not owe.

When we begin to feel fear, we look around for something *to* fear. Considering all there is to look at (the media, the environment, our body, our memory, our imagination), we have little trouble finding *something*. Thus the fear grows, our perception of the world darkens and it becomes an increasingly terrible place.

Sophocles (5th Century B.C.) knew this when he wrote, "To him who is in fear, everything rustles."

Eventually, we begin to avoid all things and thoughts that even *might* produce fear, or that *might* produce the fear of fear, or that *might* produce the fear of fear of fear. It becomes a many-layered fortress—fear defending fear defending fear defending fear—and inside: nothing.

It is one of the great jokes of existence. When people take the courage to journey into the center of their fear, they find—nothing. It was only many layers of fear, being afraid of itself.

This realization is either tragic or comic. When people experience this, they are often seen laughing and crying simultaneously—and the unenlightened nearby may fear that they have gone mad.

When unreal fears become extreme, it's known as paranoia. As Tennessee Williams warned an interviewer,

Fear is that little darkroom
where negatives are developed.

MICHAEL PRITCHARD

"I'm a paranoic, baby, so I hope you don't make the mistake of laboring under the false impression that you are talking to a sane person."

Anytime we let unreal fears (and that includes untested fears) keep us from moving toward our dreams, it is a form of madness. If the madness makes us furious, that might not be so bad: "To be furious is to be frightened out of fear." (Shakespeare, yet again.) But for most, the insanity of fear only produces discomfort and inaction.

And more fear.

Hail to you gods,
On that day of the great reckoning.
Behold me, I have come to you,
Without sin, without guilt, without evil,
Without a witness against me,
Without one whom I have wronged.
I am one pure of mouth, pure of hands.

THE BOOK OF THE DEAD
THE ADDRESS TO THE GODS
1700-1000 B.C.
(NOT USED IN SEVERAL CENTURIES—OBVIOUSLY)

We find the defendants incredibly guilty.

THE FOREMAN RETURNING THE VERDICT ON
ZERO MOSTEL AND GENE WILDER IN MEL BROOKS'
THE PRODUCERS

Guilt

Guilt is the anger we feel toward ourselves when we do something "wrong." The trouble is, most of us haven't really explored what we think is truly "right" and "wrong" in years—maybe ever.

Even if we *have* explored our own sense of right and wrong, feeling guilty for things we don't personally think are wrong often prevails. It's a habit. So, even if we know guilt is a waste of time, we feel it anyway. Then we feel guilty about *that*.

Guilt is something we get so *clever* about. We always seem to be able to find subtler and subtler levels of self-judgement. "The only reason I still feel guilty about masturbation," David Steinberg said, "is that I do it so badly."

The process of limitation and immobility is *fear before* we do something new, and *guilt after*. (Maybe that's why they're both felt in the area of the stomach.) Guilt is the remorse—the shame, the regret—we feel at having done something "different." We feel so bad we promise ourselves, "I'll never do that again!" even if it's the very thing we need to do, over and over.

When we've had enough blaming ourselves, we often find someone or something else to blame—"The devil made me do it" in all its various forms. In addition to purging the offending *action* from our lives, we also promise to avoid the person (situation, thing, etc.) that "caused" our "downfall."

And so our circle of activity becomes smaller and smaller. The comfort zone closes in.

Guilt is tricky. It's not always a deep, painful feeling—a desperate need for atonement. It has other methods. It can, for example, rewrite the *memory* of an experience. We may do something new, enjoy the doing of it (or the result of doing it), and guilt will actually convince us that we didn't like it (or got nothing from it). We can say to someone, "I'm not going to do that again; I didn't really

Last night at twelve
I felt immense,
But now I feel like thirty cents.

GEORGE ADE

1902

like it," and believe it—although, in fact, the experience itself (not the fear before the experience or the guilt after, but the *actual experience itself*) was enjoyable (or profitable).

Keep in mind we're not talking about hurting yourself or others. We're talking about the guilt we feel when we do something new (submitting a manuscript to a publisher, say, or taking a high school equivalency test) and fail. Although we learned something from the failure, guilt steps in and convinces us, "The lesson wasn't worth the cost."

We're also talking about feeling uneasy about trying something new and *succeeding*. Remember that guilt is not rational. Many of us have irrational beliefs that we should not be *too* successful. "Who do you think you are?" guilt asks, "Someone special? What's wrong with the way things are? You have no *appreciation*. Why can't you fit in? Why do you always have to do it *your way*? Can't you learn to *cooperate?*" And on and on.

It's guilt's job to make us feel bad when we violate even a *limiting* belief about ourselves. A limiting belief such as unworthiness, for example.

*You have no idea what
a poor opinion
I have of myself—
and how little I deserve it.*

W. S. GILBERT

Unworthiness

Unworthiness is the deep-seated belief we have about ourselves that tells us we're undeserving, not good enough, inadequate, and fundamentally deficient.

It's the primal doubt we feel in the pit of our stomach when we consider living a dream. "Don't try it," unworthiness warns. "Don't even *think* about it."

And so, we don't even think about it. Our mind goes off on one distraction after another—anything rather than having to face even the *possibility* of our own elemental inadequacy.

Of all the components of the comfort zone, unworthiness is the most hideous, and therefore, the most hidden—especially from ourselves. We can stand feeling *bad,* but to feel that we are lacking even the most meager spark of goodness—that we are condemned to never have what we truly want, *and, to deserve that condemnation—* is beyond pain and terror, it's unthinkable.

Even if there's the *possibility* that what unworthiness says is true, we don't want to know it. We camouflage and cover and avoid any thought about the subject. We act *as if* it *might* be true, which, eventually, convinces us that it *must* be true—otherwise, why would we spend so much time *pretending* we're good and *pretending* we're happy and *pretending* we're worthy? We'll quickly abandon the thought of fulfilling a dream if it means a momentary calming of the center, a comforting of the Doubt of Doubts.

Physically, unworthiness resides in the area of the solar plexus—an area just below the breast bone where the rib cage forms an inverted "V". In some Eastern traditions, they call this the center of *Chi,* a fundamental point for focusing energy and moving ahead in life. Unworthiness inhibits that energy.

As Abraham Lincoln pointed out, "It is difficult to make a man miserable while he feels he is worthy of himself and claims kindred to the great God who made him."

I grew up to have my father's looks,
my father's speech patterns,
my father's posture,
my father's opinions,
and my mother's
contempt for my father.

JULES FEIFFER

My vigor, vitality and cheek repel me.
I am the kind of woman
I would run from.

NANCY, LADY ASTOR

Paraphrasing Lincoln in the negative (which is what unworthiness always does): "It is easy to make a man miserable while he feels he is unworthy of himself and not good enough to claim kindred to the great God who made him."

When reading "Be free, all worthy spirits, and stretch yourselves, for greatness and for height," (George Chapman, 1608), unworthiness says, in what seems our own voice, "That obviously doesn't apply to me."

When offered something we really want, unworthiness says, "No, I couldn't."

One of the most popular of unworthiness' comments, however, is, upon hearing of our own good fortune, "I don't believe it! That's too good to be true!" It's often spoken with such enthusiasm—and such self-limitation—the good that's "unbelievable" soon disappears.

Unworthiness can destroy relationships. When we don't feel worthy, we can't love ourselves—how can we love ourselves knowing our Dark Secret? And all the games we play to cover the unworthiness—how insincere, how phony, how deceptive we are. No, we are not worthy of our love.

If someone loves us, we resent them—how can we respect anyone who falls for the facade we slapped together so haphazardly and manipulate so desperately? Anyone loving us must be easily deceived, and not worthy of our attention. Conversely, the people who dislike us we tend to (sometimes secretly) admire—they must be very wise to see to the truth of our very being.

Unworthiness forms the foundation of the comfort zone.

*I buy women shoes,
and they use them
to walk away from me.*

MICKEY ROONEY

Hurt Feelings

How much closer to living our dreams we'd all be if everyone who ever promised us something delivered. How much fuller our lives would be if, any time we asked people for something, they would say yes by giving it to us. When we don't get what we want from others, when they fail to keep their promises, when they let us down, we often have hurt feelings.

Even deeper (and more frequent) are the times we have let *ourselves* down. How much greater are our imagination and desires than our physical abilities to fulfill them.

The result of all this letdown is often hurt feelings—sadness, loss, grief.

In our bodies, hurt feelings are felt in the center of the chest, in the area most people refer to as the heart. (As with the stomach, it's not located directly over the physical heart, but close.)

A common "cover-up" for hurt is anger. We blame whatever or whoever let us down, and we get steamed. ("How *dare* you!") Some people have anger as the *automatic* response to disappointment. In almost all cases, however, hurt is just underneath.

A common defense against hurt feelings is depression. Some people feel so *down* all the time that one more hurt is just another drop in the ocean of their melancholy. (Remember, much of this is not logical, by adult standards.)

After enough hurt, anger and depression, people tend to decide, "I'm not going to do anything that causes me any more pain." That would, of course, include any behavior of a dream-fulfillment nature, because that almost certainly includes asking a lot of people (including ourselves) for a lot of things—some of which we'll get, and some of which (let's be honest: *most* of which) we won't.

*Discouragement is simply
the despair of
wounded self-love.*

FRANÇOIS DE FÈNELON

Discouragement

Over time, the result of all this fear, guilt, unworthiness, hurt feelings and anger is discouragement.

Discouragement promotes inaction, and inaction guarantees failure—a life of not living our dreams.

There is a story told of Beelzebub, who had a meeting with a few of his sub-Beelzebubs (subbubs). Beelzebub asked for ideas on the best way to keep people constantly frustrated by not being able to follow their dreams. All sorts of physical barriers were suggested by the subbubs, but Beelzebub rejected them all, citing examples of human beings overcoming one physical obstacle after another.

Finally, one of the subbubs suggested something that would keep human beings from even *attempting* to overcome the barriers between themselves and their dreams—discouragement. It was such a profound and innovative idea that Beelzebub put this subbub in charge of Strategic Planning to Make Humans Miserable. Since that time, this subbub has invented, among other things, elevator music, tamper-resistant packaging and commercials in movie theaters.

It's hard to imagine anything more pernicious—and effective—than discouragement.

When they are young, baby elephants are heavily chained to stakes driven deep in the ground. Pull as they might, they remain firmly tethered. Soon, the baby elephant becomes discouraged and stops pulling. It learns to stay put. Over time, the trainer uses lighter and lighter restraints. Eventually, a small rope attached to a stick barely anchored in the earth is sufficient to stop a fully grown elephant from moving.

In a sense, discouragement makes us all like elephants. Although we, as adults, have the power we didn't have as children to pursue our dreams, discouragement keeps us from using it.

*Why should we take up
farming when there are so
many mongongo nuts
in the world?*

AFRICAN BUSHMAN

Intermission to Part One

This section on the comfort zone is becoming downright *uncomfortable*. All these elements of the comfort zone *do* have a positive side. We'll talk about that in Part Two. In this part, however, we're talking about how people use these tools to limit themselves. It's not easy to write about, and it might not be easy to read about, but imagine how uneasy it is to continue *living* it.

So, we thought we would pause here and take a breather before going on.

Let's see...with what shall we take a breather? What fun things do we have lying around here? Ah, quotes! Yes, all those quotes we wanted to include in this book, but somehow didn't find a place for.

Quotations are comfortable. — *The Authors*

Life is like a dogsled team. If you ain't the lead dog, the scenery never changes. — *Lewis Grizzard*

I've always thought that the stereotype of the dirty old man is really the creation of a dirty young man who wants the field to himself. — *Hugh Downs*

Father, each of your sermons is better than the next. — *Anonymous churchgoer*

Destiny is not a matter of chance; it is a matter of choice. It is not a thing to be waited for; it is a thing to be achieved. — *William Jennings Bryan*

The denunciation of the young is a necessary part of the hygiene of older people, and greatly assists the circulation of the blood. — *Logan Pearsall Smith*

Eighty percent of success is showing up. — *Woody Allen*

*I don't want any
yes-men around me.
I want everybody to
tell me the truth
even if it costs them their jobs.*

SAMUEL GOLDWYN

Almost every man wastes part of his life in attempts to display qualities which he does not possess. — *Samuel Johnson*

Once you accept your own death all of a sudden you're free to live. You no longer care about your reputation. You no longer care except so far as your life can be used tactically—to promote a cause you believe in.— *Saul Alinsky*

It matters not whether you win or lose; what matters is whether I win or lose. — *Darin Weinberg*

My idea of an agreeable person is a person who agrees with me. — *Benjamin Disraeli*

Good behavior is the last refuge of mediocrity. — *Henry S. Haskins*

God is really only another artist. He invented the giraffe, the elephant, the ant. He has no real style. He just goes on trying other things. — *Pablo Picasso*

Not as bad as you might have imagined. — *Motto suggested for New Jersey by Calvin Trillin*

Having your book turned into a movie is like seeing your oxen turned into bouillon cubes. — *John LeCarre*

I've been promoted to middle management. I never thought I'd sink so low. — *Tim Gould*

Condoms aren't completely safe. A friend of mine was wearing one and got hit by a bus. — *Bob Rubin*

A "Bay Area Bisexual" told me I didn't quite coincide with either of her desires. — *Woody Allen*

Your request for no MSG was ignored. — *Fortune Cookie*

*Cats are intended to teach us
that not everything in nature
has a function.*

GARRISON KEILLOR

Advice to expectant mothers: you must remember that when you are pregnant, you are eating for two. But you must remember that the other one of you is about the size of a golf ball, so let's not go overboard with it. I mean, a lot of pregnant women eat as though the other person they're eating for is Orson Welles. — *Dave Barry*

Don't try to take on a new personality; it doesn't work. — *Richard Nixon*

Life is to be lived. If you have to support yourself, you had bloody well better find some way that is going to be interesting. And you don't do that by sitting around wondering about yourself. — *Katherine Hepburn*

When I can no longer bear to think of the victims of broken homes, I begin to think of the victims of intact ones. — *Peter De Vries*

Go to the zoo and enlist. Shave your neighbor's dog. Yo! Dump your spaghetti on that guy's head. — *Inside the ears of crazy people as observed by Gary Larson*

When I played pro football, I never set out to hurt anybody deliberately...unless it was, you know, important, like a league game or something. — *Dick Butkus*

I'm not a vegetarian because I love animals; I'm a vegetarian because I hate plants. — *A. Whitney Brown*

If at first you don't succeed, find out if the loser gets anything. — *Bill Lyon*

My wife and I were happy for twenty years. Then we met. — *Rodney Dangerfield*

Please give me some good advice in your next letter. I promise not to follow it. — *Edna St. Vincent Millay*

*I learned the way
a monkey learns—
by watching its parents.*

QUEEN ELIZABETH II

Childhood: The Psychological Basis of the Comfort Zone

No, this is not going to be one of those chapters in which our parents are blamed for *everything* we are and are not. As Russell Bishop pointed out, "I don't know any parents who look into the eyes of a newborn baby and say, 'How can we screw this kid up?'"

Our parents (or whoever raised us) *loved* us—in the most fundamental sense of that term. Maybe they didn't hug us all we wanted, but they *fed* us, *clothed* us and physically nurtured us such that we are at least alive today.

The major reasons parents don't raise their children free from trauma are:

1. *Parents don't know any better.* Children learn by example as much as anything else. If parents *knew* how to live their own lives better, they would—and that learning would be passed onto the child.

2. *Children require different rules than adults.* Children are not as capable as adults. The less capable we are, the more rules we need.

3. *Parents have other things to do besides raising children.* Making a living, keeping house, maintaining the relationship with their spouse, dealing with *their* parents, etc. Life can be overwhelming even *without* children.

4. *Who on earth knows what a child needs when?* Some complain their parents ruined them by not enough attention—they needed more loving; others claim their parents gave too much attention—they needed more freedom. Many complain about *both*. To give us precisely what we wanted, precisely when we wanted it, our parents would have had to be psychic—which some children would have considered painfully intrusive.

*I owe my success
to having listened respectfully
to the very best advice,
and then going away
and doing the exact opposite.*

G. K. CHESTERTON

Given this preamble, let's look at childhood—the place where we learned to use the elements of the comfort zone to limit ourselves.

Fear. Children don't know the difference between playing in the street and playing on a playground, between drinking poison and drinking milk, between petting the nice neighbor's cat and petting the nasty neighbor's pit bull. In order to let us out of their sight, parents must teach us not to do things that might cause us physical harm. Their tool is fear.

In turning children loose on the world (and vice-versa), the basic message from parents is, "Don't do anything I haven't personally shown you how to do." In other words, "Don't do anything new." While most of the "new" a child could do is perfectly safe, a small percentage of it is deadly, and that small percentage is what the parents want to protect the child from.

Guilt. Naturally, children ignore the cautionary statements of parents—they do what they want to do when they want to do it. Curiosity is more important than rules. So, the parents "lay down the law." (Actually, the law already *has* been laid down; now they're laying down the *punishment.)*

Punishment can include yelling (the perceived removal of love), deprivation (of freedom, food, toys, etc.), or physical pain. From a *parent's* point of view, this may not be much, but from a *child's* point of view, this can be devastating.

To children, parents are (A) real big (imagine someone thirty feet tall, weighing a thousand pounds); (B) the source of love, caring, comfort, dry diapers, etc.; and (C) the ones who protect them from all those *other* thirty-foot, thousand-pound monsters. In addition to all that, parents control the *food.*

Little wonder, then, that when parents exact punishment—even though they're doing it for "our own good"—the child reacts strongly. Sometimes it hates the parents, and sometimes it hates itself for doing whatever it did to

If you want a place in the sun,
you must leave the shade
of the family tree.

OSAGE SAYING

provoke the parent's wrath. When the latter happens, it's called guilt.

Hence, we learn to use fear as a reason not to do anything new, and if we do it anyway, to feel guilty afterwards.

Unworthiness is programmed in at the same time. If the child plays for two hours within its parent's comfort zone (toys in the living room, for example), all is well. There is little interaction with the parents; they're reading or watching TV or whatever parents do when their children are being "good." When the child goes beyond its parent's comfort zone and starts playing with, say, a can of shoe polish, the interaction with the parents becomes suddenly intensified—and almost entirely negative. Bad, wrong, nasty, naughty, no good.

What does the child remember from an evening at home with "the folks"? The hours of harmonious play, worthy of a Rockwell painting? Or the moments of intense, negative interaction? The intensity, probably. After enough memories of a negative kind, it's little wonder that a child builds an image of itself as being bad, wrong, nasty, naughty and no good. Sometimes lack of self esteem is rooted in this type of ambivalent behavior by parents.

Hurt feelings. From a very early age, we are taught that what happens *outside* us should affect what happens *inside* us. Someone jangles keys, and that's supposed to make us fascinated. Someone makes faces and silly noises, and that's supposed to make us happy. Someone gives us a Teddy bear, and that's supposed to make us feel loved. Eventually, our inner good feelings are linked to external distractions. When the distractions are not there, we feel deserted, alone, unloved.

We also learn by watching. Father arrives late, mother's feelings are hurt. Mother doesn't cook father's favorite food, father's feelings are hurt. And so on. Mother's choice in food has some *direct connection* to father's emotional condition. Must be the way it should be.

Help!
I'm being held prisoner by my heredity and environment!

DENNIS ALLEN

The Fight or Flight Response: The Physiological Basis of the Comfort Zone

Human beings, as a species, have an in-built, automatic, biological response to perceived danger: to fight like hell or to run like hell. It's called The Fight or Flight Response.

The cave dwellers who could outfight the neighbors and outrun the tigers prevailed. Those who could not became trophies and tigerfood.

In a survival-of-the-fittest sense, we are the offspring of the fittest. For the most part, the fittest were the ones who could fight the fiercest or run the fastest—or both (preferably at the same time). We inherited that. It's genetic.

The emotion of fight is anger; the emotion of flight is fear. Anger and fear—the two emotional mainstays of the comfort zone.

The key word in the definition of the fight or flight response is *perceived* danger. We don't have to actually *be* in danger to trigger the fight or flight response, we merely have to *perceive* danger. Given the power of our imagination, that's not hard to do.

Once the fight or flight response is triggered, it becomes self-perpetuating. Fear feeds anger and anger feeds fear, and both fire the imagination to "perceive" new dangers which stoke the fear-and-anger fires. Some people haven't been *out* of the fight or flight response for *years*.

It's little wonder, then, that we look for any degree of comfort we can find—even at the cost of our dreams. As Alexander Solzhenitsyn explained it, "Human beings yield in many situations, even important and spiritual and central ones, as long as it prolongs one's well-being."

*I don't want to achieve immortality
through my work.
I want to achieve it through not dying.*

WOODY ALLEN

*Either this man is dead or my
watch has stopped.*

GROUCHO MARX

Death: The Ultimate Discomfort

Beneath the psychological programming is the physiological fight or flight response, and beneath all *that* is The Big One: *death*.

Death is so final, so ultimate—so *mysterious*. ("The grand perhaps," as Robert Browning called it.) It doesn't just *feed* the various aspects of the comfort zone, it positively *inspires* them. (Dare we say it gives them life? No, we daren't.)

Fear. One small misstep, and boom—we're history. Job called it "The king of terrors" (18:14). As Professor Sydney Hook said, "Fear of death has been the greatest ally of tyranny past and present." To quote the proverb, "It is better to be a coward for a minute than to be dead the rest of your life."

Anger. The unfairness of death can make us furious. As Mel Brooks explained, "Why do we have to die? As a kid you get nice little white shoes with white laces and a velvet suit with short pants and a nice collar and you go to college, you meet a nice girl and get married, work a few years and then you have to *die!* What is this shit? They never wrote that in the contract!"

Guilt. Somehow, no matter when we die, we know we'll have *something* to do with it. We'll drive too fast or eat the wrong thing or ignore our intuition. It will probably be doing something our mothers told us not to do. Even if we repent, it's hopeless. As Johnny Carson said, "I know a man who gave up smoking, drinking, sex and rich food. He was healthy right up to the time he killed himself."

Unworthiness. If being alive is the ultimate proof of worthiness, then death must be the ultimate proof of unworthiness. No matter how much good we do, no matter how many lives we save or starving mouths we feed, someday we wind up dead.

Hurt Feelings. To lose someone or something you love hurts. Imagine how much losing *everyone* and *everything* all

Do not fear death so much,
but rather the inadequate life.

BERTOLT BRECHT

at the *same time* would hurt. No, don't imagine it. It's too uncomfortable.

Discouragement. No matter how much we build up, no matter what we acquire, no matter...what's the point of finishing this sentence—we're just going to *die* someday anyway. And everybody who reads it is going to die someday, too. So what's the point in finishing this paragraph? In fact, what's the point in finishing this chapter?

*He not busy being born
is busy dying.*

BOB DYLAN

The Bad News about the Comfort Zone

The comfort zone is never static. It is either expanding or contracting. If you're not consciously expanding the comfort zone, it contracts.

In the heating
and air conditioning trade,
the point on the thermostat in
which neither heating nor
cooling must operate
—around 72 degrees—
is called
"The Comfort Zone."
It's also known as
"The Dead Zone."

RUSSELL BISHOP

The Worst News about the Comfort Zone

The comfort zone is not just a collection of "uncomfortable" emotions—it has its own personality, character and individuality. It is a complex psychological-physiological entity unto itself.

If this sounds like some sort of science fiction horror story, you should see the horror the comfort zone wreaks on people's lives.

Many don't see the comfort zone as a limitation at all. They call it "intuition," "morality," or "conscience." Some connect it with religion—they think the limiting rantings of the comfort zone are the voice of God.

(We won't even discuss what happens when these people put their self-limitations on others—by force, if necessary. Well, take a look at history; take a look *around!*)

The comfort zone knows us intimately and hits us at our weakest point. It wouldn't dream of using an excuse we could see through. It uses the reasons we find reasonable, the rationales we find rational (the rational lies), the realizations we find most real (real lies). It takes our greatest aspirations and turns them into excuses for not bothering to aspire.

Only two things are infinite,
the universe
and human stupidity,
and I'm not sure
about the former.

ALBERT EINSTEIN

The Even Worse News about the Comfort Zone

To the degree we're not living our dreams, our comfort zone has more control of us than we have over ourselves.

Love your enemies
just in case
your friends turn out to be
a bunch of bastards.

R. A. DICKSON

The Very Worst News about the Comfort Zone

In order to truly master the comfort zone, we have to learn to love it.

*I once complained to my
father that I didn't seem to be
able to do things the same
way other people did.
Dad's advice?
"Margo, don't be a sheep.
People hate sheep.
They eat sheep."*

MARGO KAUFMAN

PART TWO

BUILT FOR SUCCESS

(Programmed for Failure, Perhaps, but)

BUILT FOR SUCCESS

Life moves on, whether we act as
cowards or heroes.
Life has no other
discipline to impose,
if we would but realize it,
than to accept life unquestioningly.
Everything we shut our eyes to,
everything we run away from,
everything we deny,
denigrate or despise,
serves to defeat us in the end.
What seems nasty, painful, evil,
can become a source of beauty, joy
and strength,
if faced with an open mind.
Every moment is a golden one
for him who has the vision
to recognize it as such.

HENRY MILLER

The Good News about the Comfort Zone

The good news about the comfort zone is that all the energy that makes up the comfort zone is *yours*.

Fear, guilt, unworthiness, hurt feelings and anger are, of course, *emotions*. *Emotion* is *energy* in *motion*. We take *our energy* and put it in *motion*. Sometimes it's joy, sometimes it's sorrow; sometimes it's guilt, sometimes it's pride; sometimes it's pain, sometimes it's pleasure—whatever the emotion, the energy that's in motion *is what we put in motion.*

People often want to "get rid of" a "negative" emotion—fear, say, or unworthiness—before attempting something new. That's the same thing as saying, "I want to get rid of some of my energy."

As we tend to get what we want, a portion of our energy is taken from us. We may not feel as much fear, guilt, unworthiness, hurt feelings or anger—but we don't have much energy, either. "I'd sure like some more energy," we say, and we get it—often in the form of fear, guilt, unworthiness, hurt feelings and anger. Then we ask for those to go away, and the cycle continues.

Fear, guilt, unworthiness, hurt feelings and anger are, in fact, *tools*. Tools are neutral—they can be used either for us, or against us. A knife can be used to heal or to hurt. A hammer can be used to build or to destroy. It is not the tool itself, but *the way the tool is used* that determines its benefit or detriment.

The difficulty lies in a fundamental *misperception* of the so-called "limiting" emotions. The limitation is not in the emotions themselves, but in the way we've been taught to *perceive* these emotions. We've been programmed with certain attitudes about certain feelings, and in the *attitudes* lie the limitations, not in the feelings.

In a sense, we play isometrics with our feelings and our attitudes. A certain feeling arises. An attitude says we

*They shall beat their swords
into plowshares, and their
spears into pruninghooks:
nation shall not lift up sword
against nation, neither shall
they learn war any more.*

ISAIAH 2:4

shouldn't have that feeling, and pushes it down. It's like arm wrestling with ourselves—we can expend a lot of energy and work diligently, but not much is accomplished. When we see how little gets done, we wonder (A) why so little was accomplished ("I tried *so hard*"), (B) why we're so tired, or (C) both.

The good news is that both the energy pushing up and the energy pushing down is *our* energy. Imagine moving toward a goal and not just *removing* the inner resistance to achieving that goal, but *adding* all the energy that was part of the resistance to the forward motion of achievement. Whew!

Imagine if all the energy of fear, guilt, unworthiness, hurt feelings and anger were available to help us achieve anything we wanted.

Well, they are.

Using fear, guilt, unworthiness, hurt feelings and anger as allies in the journey toward our dreams is not difficult. It is a matter of *understanding* their true use and function—and *remembering* that we now know their true use and function. (The habit of treating them as "the enemies" to be "gotten rid of" can be strong.)

It's as though someone hung a large rock around our neck. "Oh, how heavy," we'd complain. Later we were told the rock was really a diamond in the rough. "Oh! How heavy!" we'd exclaim.

Fear, guilt, unworthiness, hurt feelings and anger are diamonds in the rough. They're valuable now, and with a little cutting and polishing, they become priceless.

The next few chapters reveal these gems for what they are, and the rest of this book discusses various cutting and polishing techniques.

And neither shall we learn to war with ourselves any more.

*It's all right to have
butterflies in your stomach.
Just get them to fly
in formation.*

DR. ROB GILBERT

Fear Is the Energy to Do Your Best in a New Situation

Think about entering a new situation. To meet that situation, imagine that you received an extra burst of energy, your senses sharpened, and there was a tingling—an excitement—in your body, and you became more sensitive and aware.

Doesn't that sound great? The very thing we need to do our best in a new situation! Well, it's precisely what *does* happen each time we enter a new situation. Most of the time, however, we call it "fear" and we don't like it.

Contrary to popular belief, our parents didn't teach us to feel fear. Our parents *did* teach us to use fear as a reason *not* to do something. As we explained earlier, they did this from love. Children cannot logically determine if their physical well-being is or is not endangered when attempting each new activity.

Unfortunately, at eighteen-or-so when we *do* know the difference between that which is truly dangerous and that which is merely new and untried, no one draws us aside and says, "That fear you've been using as a reason *not* to do things—it's *really* part of the energy to get things done."

The first thing we need when entering a new situation (be it physically, or in our imagination) is more energy. A new situation, by definition, will be *different,* and extra energy will help us meet the challenges of whatever "different" may offer.

When we feel fear, our body releases into the bloodstream adrenaline, glucose and other energy-producing chemicals. This physical energy is available to support our thoughts and actions.

In a new situation, naturally we want all the information we can get. This is when the sharpened senses, sensitivity and heightened awareness associated with fear are useful—they help us absorb and more quickly process the new information.

*You gain strength, courage
and confidence by every
experience in which you really
stop to look fear in the face.
You are able to say to yourself,
"I lived through this horror.
I can take the next thing
that comes along."
You must do the thing you
think you cannot do.*

ELEANOR ROOSEVELT

Another aspect of fear is *letting go of irrelevancies*. We automatically focus on what's most important, "and let the rest of the world go by." When in a new situation, we want to focus on what's in front of us, what's central, what's significant. Fear drives thoughts about whether the grapefruit will be on sale or not right out of our awareness.

Part of doing our best in a new situation involves learning. There is so much to learn from a new experience—so much to learn about the experience and, more importantly, so much to learn about ourselves. Fear provides a good environment for learning—not an *ideal* environment (fear is not known for its abundance of patience)—but a *good* environment nonetheless. The energy, clarity of mind and ability to focus are excellent tools for learning.

Ultimately, we'll automatically know and use fear as the energy to do our best. In the interim—as we break the habit of thinking of this energy as a reason not to do anything new—the suggestion is: feel the fear and do it anyway.

Once you know something is not physically dangerous, go ahead and *do* the thing. It may feel uncomfortable (count on it), but keep moving one step after another in the direction of doing it. As you move—as you *use it*—the energy will transform itself from barrier to blessing. You'll have *energy*, not limitation.

This process of feeling the fear and doing it anyway reprograms our attitude from, "Fear means, 'Don't' " to "Fear means, 'All systems go!' "

*My parents have been visiting
me for a few days.
I just dropped them off
at the airport.
They leave tomorrow.*

MARGARET SMITH

Guilt Is the Energy for Personal Change

Guilt is anger directed toward ourselves, and anger is the energy for *change*.

Alas, few of us were trained to use anger for change (except, perhaps, in athletics). Mostly, we use anger for *blame* and *feeling bad*. The gift of anger, however, is the physical, mental and emotional strength to make change.

When we feel guilty, and want to use the anger for change (for a change), we have two options: we can either change our *actions,* or change our *beliefs* about those actions.

As the old saying goes, "When you get sick and tired of being tired and sick, you'll change." When angry, people often say, "I'm sick and tired of this!" The question is, how sick and how tired do we need to get before we change?

When we feel guilty about something, sometimes we can change the action, sometimes we can't. If we feel guilty about something that hasn't yet happened (that twinge of guilt we feel when premeditating a "wicked" action), we can use the anger to *not* do it (or, if it's a guilt of omission, to do it).

If we feel guilty about something that's already taken place, we can use the anger to make amends, to clean things up (atonement, which leads to at-one-ment).

If there's nothing we can do, then we can use the energy of guilt to change the *belief* about how bad, wicked, terrible, immoral, despicable, disgusting and downright slug-like our action was.

Most people use guilt to (A) make half-hearted (but often heated) promises to "never do it again," which they don't really believe any more than anyone else who has known them for any length of time, and/or (B) feel bad.

Feeling bad is a very important part in the *mis*use of guilt. Part of the "contract" for violating our beliefs is that we feel bad. The sentence we tell ourselves is something

When such as I cast out remorse
So great a sweetness flows
into the breast
We must laugh and
we must sing,
We are blest by everything,
Everything we look upon is blest.

WILLIAM BUTLER YEATS

like, "Good people are _____ (fill in the perfect human behavior violated by the contrary action), *and when they're not, they feel guilty.*"

In this limiting system, feeling guilty *proves* goodness. Good people feel bad when they do something bad. (After all, bad people feel *good* when they do something bad.) So, guilt allows us to maintain a mistaken (but good-sounding) belief about ourselves *while* acting in such a way that violates that belief.

The more productive use of the energy is to *change the belief*. Once the belief is changed (and it may take many repetitions to do so), the self-judgements stop—the energy is no longer directed toward feeling bad when doing (or failing to do) certain activities.

We're not saying change your belief about yourself from "I am a good person..." to "I am a bad person..." We're saying, add a modifier to whatever belief you have about yourself, "...and sometimes they're not (don't, do, etc.)." "Good people are always kind to others...and sometimes they're not." "Good people always stick to their diet...and sometimes they don't." "Good people never yell in public...and sometimes they do."

As B. F. Skinner pointed out, "Society attacks early, when the individual is helpless."

The habit of feeling guilty over certain things—and the habit of feeling guilty *period*—is deep seated, instilled before we can understand language, much less understand. It takes great energy and perseverance to change it.

Fortunately, there's a lot of energy available in the anger of guilt. It's a matter of remembering to redirect it from *blame* to *change—over and over.*

The question arises, "When do we use the energy to change the *action,* and when do we use it to change the *belief* about the action?"

The wages of sin are death,
but by the time
taxes are taken out,
it's just sort of a tired feeling.

PAULA POUNDSTONE

That's an important question. Here are some thoughts on it.

1. If you change the *belief* first, changing the *action* is easier. So, even if you want to change the action, taking the pressure off by changing the belief might allow for the freedom of movement necessary to change the action.

2. Realize you're not going to change all the actions about which you currently feel guilty. We're not perfect, we're human. Nonetheless, in our childhood we are given images of perfection to live up to. We add to these the perfect images we have as adults. We'll discuss this "perfection syndrome" later, but for now realize that, to paraphrase ourselves, "You can change *anything* you want, but you can't change *everything* you want."

3. Change first the things that *physically harm* others. We're not talking about hurting someone's *feelings;* we're talking about activities such as hitting people, stealing, child abuse, drunk driving, etc., in which another is *physically* harmed by your actions.

4. Change next the actions that *physically harm* you. Smoking, extreme overeating, high-risk sexual activities, drug or alcohol abuse, and so on. Again, these are not the things that might *emotionally* harm you (that's quite often the comfort zone popping up and saying, "Let's take care of ourself and not change this!"), but things that *physically* do you harm.

5. Later in the book, you'll have the opportunity to make a list of your wants, desires and dreams, then to prioritize them in such a way that you'll know which you have time to pursue, and which you (for now) do not. Work next on changing the actions that go against your primary goals.

*Everything I did in my life
that was worthwhile
I caught hell for.*

EARL WARREN

6. If you've handled *all those* and are *still* looking for more, well, you're a better person than we are, Gunga Din!

☆

When used to produce guilt, the statement, "I could have done better!" is false. If we *knew* better we'd *do* better.

We don't just mean *intellectually* knowing better—our perfectionism is an intellectual process. In our mind, we often "know" better—or *think* we do. Alas, as you've probably noticed, something happens (or fails to happen) when the perfection gets from "in here" to "out there."

We're talking about *knowing* in the full sense of the word—the way you *know* to walk, talk and breathe. Yes, we sometimes have trouble with those, but, for the most part, people demonstrate their knowledge of these things through *action*.

A more accurate statement when we *intellectually* knew better (and did it anyway) is to say, "This will remind me to do better next time—I'm still learning." Because, of course, we are.

There are three reasons why lawyers are replacing rats as laboratory research animals. One is that they're plentiful, another is that lab assistants don't get attached to them, and the third is that there are some things rats just won't do.

Unworthiness Keeps Us On Track

Just as "We can have *anything* we want, we just can't have *everything* we want," so, too, we are *worthy* of anything we want, we just may not be worthy of everything we want.

Why? Unless our list of wants is truly meager, or, unless we plan to live forever, we simply don't have the *time* to fulfill them all. (More on this later in the chapter, *You Can Have Anything You Want, You Just Can't Have Everything You Want.*)

Say we want to be a lawyer (God knoweth why, but let's suppose for the sake of an example we do), we commit to being a lawyer, and begin actions toward becoming a lawyer. One day, if we think, "I'd like to be a doctor," we might feel unworthiness. While studying law, the part of us that feels unworthy to be a doctor is *accurate*.

It's not that we wouldn't be a good doctor, or that we're not smart enough, or anything else—it's just that we *chose* something else, something else that takes a lot of time, money and perseverance. The sense of unworthiness about being a doctor keeps us on the lawyer track.

Even if we *did* declare a double-major—the nightmare of the insurance industry—and were (very) busy becoming an M.D., Esq., then feelings of unworthiness about being a nuclear physicist would be accurate. Even if we declared a *triple* major...well, you get the idea.

Somewhere along the line, our plate will be full. At that time, everything *not* on our plate we are unworthy of. When it's full, the way to create worthiness for more is to clear a spot on the plate.

Someone who is already a lawyer could feel more worthiness about becoming a doctor than someone who is still in law school. A practicing lawyer, as compared to a law student, has more time, more experience, and lots more money.

When you know your dream, know that you are worthy of that dream. Tell yourself you are worthy of that dream. Program that worthiness in. (Lots of techniques

The important thing in acting
is to be able to laugh and cry.
If I have to cry,
I think of my sex life.
If I have to laugh,
I think of my sex life.

GLENDA JACKSON

for that later.) Act upon that worthiness. Be content knowing that your dream is yours, and accept that everything that's not your dream is not yours.

Worthiness and unworthiness keep us on our path. It is our path. We selected it—it leads to our dream. Unworthiness is a friend that says, "Your path is this way, not that way."

If we listen and move back onto our path, we feel worthy again. If we continue to stray, we will continue to feel unworthy until we (A) get back on the path, or (B) choose another dream and another path. If we do the latter, and then attempt to get back on the "old" path, unworthiness will remind you, "This is not your path anymore."

Seen in this way, the feeling of unworthiness is better described as *humility*. We know what we want, we know the direction we're going, we know that we are entitled to our dream, and we let the rest of the goals go by.

Humility comes with maturity. Children want this and this and this and this and that—practically everything they see, smell, touch or hear. Many adults do the same thing with goals—"I want a career *and* a marriage *and* children *and* a house *and* a car *and* save the whales *and* stop pollution *and* write a book *and* find God. Then, next week, I want..."

It's little wonder that unworthiness is what these people fear the most and hide from the most; they feel unworthy—accurately so—quite often.

We'll talk soon about how to select which dreams to pursue, and which to consider "good ideas I might get to someday." (In other words, which you choose to be worthy of and which you do not.)

Remember—the choice of which to be worthy is *yours*.

*Don't go around saying
the world owes you a living;
the world owes you nothing;
it was here first.*

MARK TWAIN

Hurt Feelings are a Reminder of How Much We Care; Anger is the Energy for Change

Beneath hurt is caring. The depth of the hurt indicates the depth of the caring. The anger that hides the hurting shows the degree of caring, too.

We only hurt about things we care about. Yes, when anger covers the hurt we say, "I don't care about them; I *hate* them." That's part of the caring, too.

If we want A, and B stops us from having it, it's not that we "secretly" care about B. We still love A. It's easy to get lost in the hurting and hating of B, however, and forget about the caring we have for A.

Hurt feelings are a reminder to find A, refocus on A, feel the caring you have for A, and find alternate ways to get A, even if B, C, D, E and F get in the way.

Another word for caring, of course, is love. Love is powerful. Keep it directed toward your goal. Most people use hurt as a reason to stop. Then you truly *are* hurt; you hurt yourself—you keep yourself from attaining your heart's desire. You do that by stopping.

Feel the *passion* of the caring. Put that behind your goal. If you feel *anger*, remember this is the energy for change. *Use* it; *do* something with it. What you do may or may not work. If it does work, great. If not, you've learned something—probably lots of things. If nothing else, you've learned one more thing that won't work. Even if you can't do anything physically, use the energy to *imagine* success.

Another excellent use for hurt and anger is to change the *beliefs* we have about the way the world *should* treat us. As with guilt, the reason we feel hurt and anger when things and people outside us let us down is because we *believe* those things and people *shouldn't*. Well, sorry, that's not life on Earth.

Vex not thy spirit
at the course of things;
they heed not thy vexation.
How ludicrous and outlandish
is astonishment
at anything that may happen
in life.

MARCUS AURELIUS

Add "...and sometimes they don't (won't, can't, etc.)" to each belief about others that includes "should," "must," "have-to," "ought-to," or "supposed-to." It not only makes life easier, it also makes changing it easier, too.

Hurt feelings and anger—like fear, guilt and unworthiness—are there as energy to be used *toward* your goal, not as reasons to stop.

Our *feelings* don't say stop—our *programming* says stop. It's time to rewrite that programming to say, "Here's the information and the energy necessary to course-correct and continue moving toward our dreams."

*The great French Marshall
Lyautey once asked his gardener
to plant a tree.
The gardener objected that the
tree was slow growing and
would not reach maturity
for 100 years.
The Marshall replied,
"In that case, there is no time
to lose; plant it this afternoon!"*

JOHN F. KENNEDY

Death—The Ultimate Deadline

Deadlines help us get things done, and there's no greater—or more certain, or more final—deadline than death. Deadlines get us going, get us moving, motivate us to do things sooner rather than later.

Parkinson's Law states that work either expands or contracts to fill the time available. Death lets us know that there's only a certain amount of time available—the span of a lifetime—in which to get done whatever we want to do.

Of course, none of us knows how *short* that time will be, but most of us know it's not going to be longer than, say, another 100 years. So, whatever we want to achieve during our lifetime, we had better start today.

There are some who consider both death and deadlines bad. Death is neither good nor bad, it merely *is*. It is a fact of life, like gravity. ("Gravity isn't easy, but it's the law.") We can use death *for* ourselves or *against* ourselves. The choice is ours.

As Professor Sydney Hook pointed out, "The fear of death has been the greatest ally of tyranny past and present." The first step in seeing death as an ally of accomplishment is to remove the childhood fears we have concerning death.

Children learn about death in a limited (and limiting) way. They see someone (or, in the case of a pet, something) go from warm, active, moving and alive, to cold, inactive, motionless and dead. This death stuff does not look very interesting.

Children then see the reaction adults have to death. Although grown-ups may *say* things like, "He is with God," or "She is at peace at last," the emotional *attitudes* of adults (weeping, moaning, wailing) indicate that death is not a welcome guest in anyone's home.

The last straw for children concerns what happens to bodies. If a body is buried, the child thinks death must be

In the last analysis it is our
conception of death which decides our
answers to all the questions
that life puts to us.

DAG HAMMARSKJÖLD

Death is nature's way of saying,
"Your table is ready."

ROBIN WILLIAMS

eternal blackness, darkness and aloneness. If a body is cremated, the child thinks death is fire, flames and pain.

For children, asking adults about death is about as useful as asking adults about sex—the adults become uncomfortable, and give conflicting answers to simple questions they don't seem to believe themselves.

It's little wonder, then, that many children decide, "Death is not a good thing, and I won't think about it any more." And most people don't. Death is such a taboo in our culture that we don't even talk about the fact that it's a taboo. We pretend it doesn't exist.

This is too bad, because there are only three beliefs about death in our culture—none of them bad.

Life is purely biological, and when we die, we're dead. There's nothing bad in this view of death—we simply are not, so there's nothing to worry about. As Einstein explained, "The fear of death is the most unjustified of all fears, for there's no risk of accident for someone who's dead."

After life, there is heaven or hell through all eternity. If this is one's belief about what happens after death, then there's nothing to worry about, either. Heaven is for good people and hell is for bad people, and who but a good person would believe in heaven and hell? So, if you believe, then a place in heaven is already prepared for you.

We keep coming back, life after life, until we learn all we need to know. This, too, is not a view of death to fear. Death is no more significant than moving from one grade to another in the same school, or from one house to another within the same town. We may not know all that will happen there, but that's part of the fun. "Life is a great surprise," Vladimir Nabokov said, "I do not see why death should not be an even greater one."

When questioned about life and death, almost all adults will describe one of these beliefs, or a close variation. As none of these views of death are *bad* nor inherently *scary,* it's clear that the views of death formed as a child still control the emotional reactions many adults have toward death.

*Even very young children need
to be informed about dying.
Explain the concept of death
very carefully to your child.
This will make threatening
him with it much
more effective.*

P.J. O'ROURKE

Many believe that young people have no sense of death; that they live their lives as though they will live forever. This may be true in some cases, but only because they have not been taught the inevitability of death, and the value of the interval between now and the inevitable. One's own mortality need not come as a shock later in life; it can be a fact of life, taken into consideration in all of life's choices.

When seen clearly as a deadline, death can be used as a tool for doing. Some of the positive uses for this tool include:

1. When we know "our days are numbered," we see that we can only accomplish a certain amount in this lifetime. This stresses the importance of *choice* in the planning and living of life.

2. Death encourages action. We only have so much time left, so let's get going.

3. Death encourages risk. The downest of the downside in any risk is death. Since we're going to die anyway, why not take the risks that make life more exciting, enjoyable and, well, alive? Near San Francisco, a group of people with AIDS gather regularly for sky diving, rock climbing and all those things they wanted to do but at one time considered "too dangerous." The name of their organization? The What-The-Hell-Do-We-Have-To-Lose-Anyway? Club. "Life," as Guy Bellamy reminds us, "is a sexually transmitted disease."

4. Death reminds us how much we owe the past and the future. Those who went before us knew they wouldn't be here forever, and yet they left us a rich legacy. We, too, have many gifts to leave the generations yet unborn. Death says we only have a certain number of years in which to appreciate the past and to leave our gift for the future. When Isaac Asimov, who has written hundreds of books, was asked what he would do if he had only six months to live, he responded, "Type faster."

Death, for the doer, is the ultimate reason to do it—and to enjoy it—*now*.

*Courage is doing
what you're afraid to do.
There can be no courage
unless you're scared.*

EDDIE RICKENBACKER

Discouragement Reveals Our Courage

Imagine how powerful discouragement is: thus far it's kept us from our dreams. The power of discouragement is available for obtaining our goals (or illuminating a small Southern town) by simply dismissing the *dis* from *discouragement*.

Courage, contrary to popular belief, is not the *absence* of fear. Courage is the wisdom to act *in spite of* fear. In time, courage becomes the ability to use all the elements of the comfort zone as additional energy to move toward our goal. When we add *en* to courage, we have *encourage*. *En* is a prefix meaning "to be at one with."

We can think of encouragement as a cheerleader. Whereas discouragement says, "Give up! Give up! Give up!" encouragement says, "Keep going! Keep going! Keep going!" or "DO IT! DO IT! DO IT!" (Which is what the advertisements for this book say as well.)

Along the way, *expect* to be discouraged—to hear and to follow the voices of discouragement. That's to be expected. The goal is not to never be discouraged again. The goal is to (A) catch the discouragement sooner, (B) call it for what it is, and (C) get out of it faster. How do we get out of it? You simply call on encouragement.

Oh, encouragement!

In fact, here's a scene from the play *Oh, Encouragement!*

SCENE: YOU are about to do something new—a necessary step along the path to one of your dreams. DISCOURAGEMENT has convinced you not to take the step. You call...

YOU: Oh, encouragement!

ENCOURAGEMENT: Yes.

YOU: Over here.

ENCOURAGEMENT: I thought you'd never ask.

*Very few people possess
true artistic ability.
It is therefore both unseemly
and unproductive to irritate
the situation by
making an effort.
If you have a burning, restless
urge to write or paint,
simply eat something sweet
and the feeling will pass.*

FRAN LEBOWITZ

DISCOURAGEMENT: (Imitating your voice) I didn't ask. Stay over there where you belong.

YOU: No, encouragement. Come here! That was discouragement talking.

ENCOURAGEMENT: I know. Here I am.

DISCOURAGEMENT: (Imitating your voice) Thank you, now go away.

YOU: Don't listen; that was discouragement again.

ENCOURAGEMENT: I'm not going—and don't you listen to discouragement, either. You can do the thing you want to do. You know you can.

YOU: But I'm afraid.

DISCOURAGEMENT: You know what fear means: "Don't do it!" *Everybody* knows that.

ENCOURAGEMENT: Fear is the energy to do your best in a new situation. You're in a new situation, so, naturally, you're afraid. *Use* the energy.

YOU: Oh, right.

DISCOURAGEMENT: Oh, wrong. Besides, if you do it you'll feel guilty.

ENCOURAGEMENT: Quiet.

YOU: But discouragement is right. *I will* feel guilty.

DISCOURAGEMENT: You'll feel guilty and miserable and you'll *deserve* to feel guilty and miserable.

ENCOURAGEMENT: Guilt is anger at yourself, and anger is the energy to make changes. Is this something that hurts yourself or someone else?

DISCOURAGEMENT: Yes.

YOU: No. It's just new and different.

DISCOURAGEMENT: It'll hurt *you*.

YOU: How?

DISCOURAGEMENT: It'll hurt you *emotionally*. You shouldn't feel uncomfortable. It's dangerous. It can kill

*Every human being on this
earth is born with a tragedy,
and it isn't orginal sin.
He's born with the tragedy
that he has to grow up.
A lot of people don't have
the courage to do it.*

HELEN HAYES

you. You can have a heart attack. You can have a stroke.

ENCOURAGEMENT: Give us a break.

DISCOURAGEMENT: No. Speaking of breaks, you might break your leg, you might break your neck...

ENCOURAGEMENT: (To you) Is this step you're afraid to take moving you in the direction of your dreams?

YOU: Yes.

ENCOURAGEMENT: Then DO IT!

DISCOURAGEMENT: There you go, advertising that lousy book again. (To you) You're not worthy to do this! Who do you think you are? Do you always have to be so *special*?

ENCOURAGEMENT: Quiet.

DISCOURAGEMENT: No. I'm going to stay right here and ruin everything. It's my job, and I love it. Even if it *wasn't* my job, I'd *still* do it.

ENCOURAGEMENT: (To you) Is this a step toward your heart's desire?

DISCOURAGEMENT: No.

YOU: Yes.

ENCOURAGEMENT: Then you're worthy of it.

DISCOURAGEMENT: You'll fail.

YOU: Yeah, I might fail.

ENCOURAGEMENT: If you do, then you'll learn from the failure, but I don't think you'll fail.

DISCOURAGEMENT: You'll be let down. It will hurt your feelings. You'll feel bad, terrible, miserable, deserted.

ENCOURAGEMENT: You'll be fine. You don't have to respond to *anything* that happens to you with hurt, and, if you do, you can remember that beneath the hurt is loving. Refocus on the loving and redirect that toward your goal.

DISCOURAGEMENT: You'll be pissed off, furious, seething—you might have a heart attack.

*Our doubts are traitors,
and make us lose the good
we oft might win by
fearing to attempt.*

WILLIAM SHAKESPEARE

YOU: Heart attack!

ENCOURAGEMENT: Use the energy of anger to make a positive change. Or change the belief you have that people should treat you in a certain way. Beneath the anger is the loving. Go to the loving. You will not have a heart attack.

DISCOURAGEMENT: Will too! Will too! Will too!

ENCOURAGEMENT: Give it a rest, huh?

DISCOURAGEMENT: No, I won't.

ENCOURAGEMENT: (To you) Shall we pull out the big guns?

YOU: Sure.

DISCOURAGEMENT: No! No!

ENCOURAGEMENT: Ready?

YOU: Yes.

ENCOURAGEMENT: Set?

YOU: Uh-huh.

DISCOURAGEMENT: Wait! No!

ENCOURAGEMENT: Go!

YOU: I Love You!

DISCOURAGEMENT: Arrrgghh!

YOU: I love you! I love you!

DISCOURAGEMENT: Stop! Stop! You'll have a heart attack!

YOU: I love you! I love you! I love you!

DISCOURAGEMENT: You're crazy! I'm getting out of here. I'll come back when you've settled down. (Exits)

YOU: I love you!

ENCOURAGEMENT: OK, so let's DO IT!

YOU: There you go, advertising that book again.

The longer I live
the more I see that I am
never wrong about anything,
and that all the pains
I have so humbly taken
to verify my notions have only
wasted my time.

GEORGE BERNARD SHAW

The Imagination Is for Rehearsing Our Dreams and Reliving Our Joys

The imagination is a fascinating, powerful place. For example, remember any incident from elementary school—writing with a fat pencil, perhaps. (Remember those fat pencils?) Now, think of someplace you plan to go in the next month and imagine yourself there. Good. Now, imagine yourself on the moon, looking back at the earth— a big blue marble in the blackness of space. Excellent.

This is the power of the imagination: we can return to the past, rehearse the future, and zoom off on flights of fancy—all within seconds.

The images you had may not have been well-detailed, or held in the imagination for very long, but you probably had some sense of each. Some people primarily *see* in their imaginations, others primarily *hear*, others primarily *feel*. Whatever you do is fine.

When the comfort zone has control of the imagination, it is vigorously and creatively used *against* us. We relive the horrors of the past—the fears that were justified, the guilts that were especially foul, the unworthinesses at their worst, the hurt feelings at their most painful, the anger at its most destructive. Considering the false history created by the comfort zone's careful selection and occasional rewriting, it's easy to feel discouraged about ourselves and everything we might consider doing.

The comfort zone also uses the imagination when considering the future. It projects an image of not just failure but *monumental* failure, *embarrassing* failure, *public* and *unconditional* failure. Considering this opposition, it's amazing that we even get out of bed.

The comfort zone also uses every news story—and every other fictional account—of disaster to show us *why* we had better not do anything new, ever.

It's time to recapture the imagination from the comfort zone. Oh, sure, the comfort zone may *claim* to have

*The ancestor of every action
is a thought.*

EMERSON

complete ownership, or maybe a 99-year lease, but, in fact, it doesn't even have squatter's rights (although it's been squatting there for some time, doing what things often do when they squat).

Evict it! Out! Your imagination is yours. You can remember the past you choose, rehearse the future you want, and identify with the real and fictional heroes and events of your selection.

When we remember the good things from our past (and all our pasts are filled with both good and bad), we build an image of ourselves as doers and achievers—charmed, kind and terrific. This forms a solid base for future action.

When we project our dreams into a positive future, we see that we *can* have what we want. A positive image of the future not only shows us how to get there, it *draws* us to it, attracting us toward our dreams like a magnet.

When we hear some *good* news, read an inspirational story or see an uplifting movie, we can use our imagination to put ourselves in the center of the action. This allows us to *identify* with all the good, happy and wonderful images in our culture—and know that we're one of them.

The positive use of the imagination is often called *visualization*. The word *visual* in *visualization* does not necessarily mean "to see." *Visual* is used in the general sense, as in, "See what I mean?" As we mentioned before, some people see, while others primarily hear and others primarily feel. Any one, or any combination, is fine.

An excellent way to reclaim property is to *build* on it. We suggest building a *sanctuary*. If you haven't already built one from reading either *LIFE 101* or *You Can't Afford the Luxury of a Negative Thought*, you might want to take some time and do it now. We'll be using the sanctuary later in this book. If you do have a sanctuary, you might want to do a little revisiting—or even remodeling—as you read the next few pages.

Enjoy!

When love and skill
work together,
expect a masterpiece.

JOHN RUSKIN

The Sanctuary

A sanctuary is an inner retreat you build with visualization in your imagination. Here you can discover the truth about yourself, and work to affirm it. ("Make it firm.")

We call it a sanctuary. Some call it a workshop, or an inner classroom. You can call it whatever word gives you the sense of asylum, harbor, haven, oasis, shelter—a place you can go to learn your lessons in peace and harmony. We refer to it as a sanctuary.

There are absolutely no limits to your sanctuary, although it's a good idea to put some limits on it. In this way, the sanctuary is a transitional point between the limitations of our physical existence and unlimitedness.

The sanctuary can be any size, shape or dimension you choose—large and elaborate or small and cozy. It can be located anywhere—floating in space, on a mountain top, by an ocean, in a valley, anywhere. (You are welcome to combine all those, if you like.) The nice thing about the sanctuary: you can change it or move it anytime—instantly.

The sanctuary can contain anything you choose. We'll suggest some things here, but consider this just the beginning of your shopping list. Before giving our design tips (you can consider us interior designers—with an emphasis on the word interior), we'll talk about ways in which you might want to build your sanctuary.

Some people will build theirs by simply reading the suggestions: as they read each, it's there. Others might read them over now for information, and then put on some soft music, close their eyes and let the construction begin. Still others may want to make this an *active* process. With their eyes closed (and being careful not to bump into too much furniture), they might physically move as each area of the sanctuary is built and used. All—or any combination—of these is, of course, fine.

I can believe anything,
provided it is incredible.

OSCAR WILDE

While reading through our suggestions, you will probably get ideas for additions or alterations. By all means make notes of these, or simply incorporate them as you go. Have we gotten across the idea that this is *your* sanctuary? OK, let's go.

Entryway. This is a door or some device that responds only to you and lets only you enter. (We'll suggest a way to bring others into your sanctuary in a moment.)

Light. Each time you enter your sanctuary, a pure, white light cascades over you, surrounding, filling, protecting, blessing and healing you—for your highest good, and the highest good of all concerned.

Main Room. Like the living room of a house or the lobby of a hotel, this is the central area. From here, there are many directions to go and many things to explore.

People Mover. This is a device to move people in and out of your sanctuary. No one ever enters without your express permission and invitation. You can use an elevator, conveyor belt, *Star Trek* beam-me-up device, or anything else that moves people. Let there be a white light at the entry of the mover as well, so that as people enter and leave your sanctuary, they are automatically surrounded, filled, protected and healed by that white light, and only that which is for their highest good and the highest good of all concerned is taking place.

Information Retrieval System. This is a method of getting any kind of information—providing, of course, it's for your highest good (and the highest good of all concerned) that you have it. The Information Retrieval System can be a computer screen, a staff of librarians, a telephone, or any other device from which you feel comfortable asking questions and getting answers.

Video Screen. This is a video (or movie, if you like) screen in which you can view various parts of your life—past, present or future. The screen has a white Light around it. When you see images you don't like or don't want to encourage, the Light is off. When the screen displays images you want to affirm, the Light glows. (Those

*I am looking for a lot of men
who have an infinite capacity
to not know what can't be done.*

HENRY FORD

who are old enough to remember Sylvania's Halo of Light television know just what we mean.)

Ability Suits. This is a closet of costumes that, when worn, give you the instant ability to do anything you want to do—great actor, successful writer, perfect lover, eager learner, Master of your Universe; any and all are available to you. When you're done with an Ability Suit, just throw it on the floor in front of the closet—Ability Suits have the ability to hang themselves up.

Ability Suit Practice Area. This is a place you can try new skills—or improve upon old ones—while wearing your Ability Suits. Leave lots of room, because there's an Ability Suit for flying and another for space travel. In your sanctuary, not even the sky's a limit.

Health Center. Here the healing arts of all the ages—past, present, future; traditional and alternative— are gathered in one place. All are devoted to your greater health. The Health Center is staffed with the most competent health practitioners visualization can buy. Who is the most healing being you can imagine? That's who runs your Center.

Playroom. Here, all the toys you ever wanted—as a child or as an adult—are gathered. There's lots of room— and time—to play with each. As with Ability Suits, you never have to worry about "putting your toys away." They put themselves away.

Sacred Room. This is a special sanctuary within your sanctuary. You can go there for meditation, contemplation or special inner work.

Master Teacher. This is your ideal teacher, the being with whom you are the perfect student. The Master Teacher (or MT for short) knows everything about you (has always been with you, in fact). The MT also knows all you need to learn, the perfect timing for your learning it, and the ideal way of teaching it to you. You don't *create* a Master Teacher—that's already been done. You *discover* your Master Teacher. To meet your Master Teacher, simply walk over to your People Mover, ask for your Master

*Advice is what we ask for
when we already know the
answer but wish we didn't.*

ERICA JONG

Teacher to come forth, and from the pure, white light of your People Mover comes your Master Teacher.

(We'll leave you two alone for a while. More uses for the Sanctuary later. See you both in the next chapter!)

Use your weaknesses;
aspire to the strength.

SIR LAURENCE OLIVIER

Newfound Friends

So, fear, guilt, unworthiness, hurt feelings and anger are really our *friends*. Hummm. That may take some getting used to. We have, for the most part, treated them as enemies. Many people have abandoned their dreams and ransomed their futures *if only* they never had to feel any of them ever again.

Yet friends they are, and friends they'll stay. Our *perception* of their friendship might not always be up to par, but they'll continue doing their friendly activities whether we realize those activities are friendly or not.

We'll be offering techniques for learning to treat these friends as friends as we go along. For now, here are some suggestions on ways to work with your newfound friends:

1. When you're using fear, guilt, unworthiness, hurt feelings or anger to limit or discourage yourself, pause and remember:

   • Fear is the energy to do our best in a new situation

   • Guilt is the energy for personal change

   • Unworthiness keeps us on track

   • Hurt feelings remind us how much we care

   • Anger is the energy for change

   • Discouragement reveals our courage

You can review the chapter for each of these if, in the midst of a comfort-zone binge, you ask, "What on *earth* do they mean by *that*?"

2. Observe your personal process of discouragement. What makes *you* give up before you even start (or shortly thereafter)?

   • What are the thoughts you think ("I'm too tired," "I'm no good at this sort of thing," etc.) when you use these emotions in a limiting way?

   • Where in your body do you feel fear? Guilt? Unworthiness? Hurt feelings? Anger? Which is your

Since nothing we intend
is ever faultless,
and nothing we attempt
ever without error,
and nothing we achieve
without some measure of
finitude and fallibility
we call humanness,
we are saved by forgiveness.

DAVID AUGSBURGER

"favorite"? Do they gang up? Which ones always appear with which others?

3. Allow yourself to see a way in which the emotion might *possibly* be useful. There's no need to *make* it useful—zap!—not just yet, anyway. (If you do, *wonderful!*) Simply be aware that a "friendly" use for this seemingly unfriendly emotion is *possible*.

4. Forgive yourself anytime you judge yourself for treating your friends as enemies. Forgive yourself anytime you judge yourself for all the things you could have done *if only* you had learned this years ago. Forgive yourself anytime for anything. (Unforgiveness is the mortar in the wall of the comfort zone.) Forgiveness is an easy process. Simply say, "I forgive myself for _____" and fill in the blank with the imagined transgression. Then say, "I forgive myself for judging myself for_____" and fill in the blank with the same transgression. Forgiving is also forgetting. Let it go. It's gone. While forgetting, remember: we're not perfect— we're human.

5. Love it all—the fear, the excitement, the guilt, the power for change, the unworthiness, the worthiness, the hurt feelings, the euphoric feelings, the anger, the movement, the discouragement, the encouragement, the whole process. It's known as life. ("Life!" as Cynthia Nelma exclaimed, "Can't live with it, can't live without it.") And when you don't love it all, love that, too.

☆

The key to all these suggestions is *awareness*. At this point, simply be *aware* of the comfort zone and its effect on you.

Soon, we'll get to *expanding* the comfort zone enough to include your dreams—and maybe even a dance floor. For now—what *is* your dream, anyway?

*Poor is the man
whose pleasures depend
on the permission of another.*

MADONNA

PART THREE

DISCOVERING AND
CHOOSING OUR DREAMS

Often, what we *really* want is hidden beneath what we've settled for. When the comfort zone doesn't allow the expanded behavior necessary to fulfill our dream, we tend to forget the dream. It's too painful otherwise.

When we know we *can* have what we want—that the comfort zone is under our control—we can remember what it is we truly want.

This section will explore the idea that we can have *anything* we want (though not *everything* we want), and offer suggestions on discovering and choosing our heart's desire.

*The only true happiness comes
from squandering ourselves
for a purpose.*

WILLIAM COWPER

1731-1800

On Purpose

People often confuse "goal" and "purpose."

A goal is something tangible; a purpose is a direction. A goal can be achieved; a purpose is fulfilled in each moment. We can set and achieve many goals; a purpose remains constant for life.

If the purpose were "West," for example, the goals while heading West (from New York, say) might include Philadelphia, Chicago, Los Angeles, Hawaii, the Philippines, Japan, Korea, China, Turkey, Spain, Portugal, Boston and New York. Many goals, same purpose. From there, although we had already traveled 25,000 miles, we would still have as much "West" to go (as much of our purpose to fulfill) as when we first began.

A second journey toward the West, again from New York, might include these goals: Detroit, St. Louis, Denver, Salt Lake City, San Francisco, Midway Islands, Mongolia, Greece, Italy, France, Ireland, Newfoundland, Nova Scotia and New York. Even after another 25,000 miles, there is still as much West to go as there was in the beginning. At any point in the journey, in fact, there was (and is) always an infinite amount of movement—and goals—available while living one's purpose.

You'll note that, even though the goals are numerous, there can be many goals within a goal, and lots of freedom within each. While in France, for example, one could travel North, South, East and West. As long as Ireland was the next major goal, even East could be a fulfillment of the purpose "West."

Looking at the life of someone whose purpose is, say, "I am a grateful giver," the goals along that purpose might include nursing home attendant, school teacher, physical therapist, writer and foundation president. These would, of course, only be *career* and *professional* goals. Marriage/family, social/political and religious/spiritual goals might interweave that life, all aligned with the purpose, "I am a grateful giver."

*Strong lives are motivated
by dynamic purposes.*

KENNETH HILDEBRAND

While goals are *chosen,* a purpose is *discovered.* Our purpose is something we have been doing all along, and will continue to do, regardless of circumstances, until the day we die.

When we refer to a "dream" in this book, we mean a goal—usually a significant goal that would, in a profound and vital way, fulfill one's purpose. As that dream is realized, another dream is chosen, and as that is satisfied, another. When we refer to "living your dreams," we mean a life of movement from dream to dream, always on purpose.

People can misdefine a purpose (as something to get to) or misdefine a goal (as something one is always doing no matter where one is), and feel frustrated about both. When people confuse "purpose" with "goal," they often have trouble reaching a goal, which can interfere with living on purpose.

Someone may think, for example, that his goal is to be "an actor." This is fine, except whenever he is acting—no matter what, where, how or with whom—his goal is fulfilled. The automatic goal-fulfillment mechanism within him says, "That's done. What's next?"

"What's next?" the actor puzzles. "I want to be an actor."

"You just acted," the goal-filler within says, "in that class you took. And very well, too."

"No. I want to be *paid* for acting." So the goal-fulfillment mechanism rallies its considerable resources and finds the actor a job as an avocado in a supermarket Vegetable-of-the-Week promotion. Pay: $250. The goal of being a paid actor having been met, the goal-setting mechanism shuts down for a while.

"Hey," the actor complains, "Why am I not getting any work?"

"You got work," says the goal-setting mechanism. "You acted. You got paid. Two goals, two goals fulfilled."

"I want *more* work."

"Want to try for carrot?" the goal-fulfillment mechanism asks. "Radishes are next week. You can go out for radish."

*The great thing in this world
is not so much where we are,
but in what direction
we are moving.*

OLIVER WENDELL HOLMES

"No. Actors have agents. I want an agent."

So, the goal-fulfillment mechanism finds an agent, and the agent finds nothing.

"I want an agent who will get me work. Regular work. Performing."

An agent is found who also manages a restaurant, and the actor gets regular work performing as a singing waiter.

"No! I want to be an actor! A *big* actor!"

So, the actor puts on 100 pounds.

The actor's problem is that he is confusing purpose with goal. If he discovered that his purpose was, say, "I am a joyful entertainer," then the week as an avocado could have been a fun-filled and fulfilling one.

It would also free him to set goals within his purpose that were clearly defined: "I want a major role in a feature film," "I want to star on a network sitcom," "I want to make $100,000 this year acting in commercials," and so on. These are the kinds of goals to which the goal-fulfillment mechanism within says, "Yes! Let's go!"

There'll be a lot more on goal setting later. For now, let's focus on the purpose. *Your* purpose.

*Nothing contributes so much
to tranquilizing the mind
as a steady purpose—
a point on which the soul
may fix its intellectual eye.*

MARY WOLLSTONECRAFT SHELLEY

(1797-1851)

What Is Your Purpose?

This is the first of several exercises in this book that involves *doing*—in this case, writing. Please decide now if you're reading this book just for information, or, if you're reading this book to make a significant improvement in your life. Although as authors we'd like to flatter ourselves that we could write a book the mere reading of which would make indispensable advancements in the lives of everyone who even brushed past it, we know that change comes through involvement, and involvement means doing. Our recommendation, then, is to *do* the exercises, starting with this one. If you read the book and later decide to do the exercises, please start with this one. It is the foundation of all the others.

To discover your purpose, get a piece of paper and start listing all your positive qualities. You might want to write each positive quality on 3x5 cards. This will make shuffling them easier later. If no 3x5 cards are handy, listing the qualities on paper will do.

(Do pick up 500-or-so 3x5 cards the next time you're out. We'll be using them later. If you're someone who tends to put off physical tasks until "later," and then never gets to them, you might want to put down this book and go get some 3x5 cards *now*. While you're out, consider your positive qualities. And have fun!)

Don't be shy listing your positive qualities. This is no time for false modesty. Are you kind? Considerate? Compassionate? Joyful? Loving? Loyal? Happy? Tender? Caring? Write them down.

A purpose usually begins with *"I am,"* followed by an attitude ("joyful" "happy" "caring") and an action ("giver" "explorer" "nurturer").

On another page (or another set of cards), start listing *actions* you find nurturing—the positive things you like doing most. Giving? Sharing? Exploring? Teaching? Learning?

*One doesn't discover new
lands without consenting to
lose sight of the shore
for a very long time.*

ANDRÉ GIDE

Take some time with this process. Reflect on your life. Explore its motivation.

If you get stuck, call a few friends and ask them for suggestions. Tell them you're filling out an application for the Peace Corps. You need help with the questions, "What are your best qualities?" and "What activities do you find give you the most satisfaction?"

You might also go to your sanctuary and ask your Master Teacher for some ideas. Or, go to the video screen and review some scenes of satisfaction, joy or fulfillment from your life. What were the qualities you embodied and the actions you performed in those situations?

Consider the people you admire most. What is it you admire about them? What qualities do they embody? Those same qualities are true about you, too, so write them down.

Eventually, a pattern will emerge on the "Qualities" and the "Actions" lists. Begin grouping qualities and actions under general headings. For you, "Compassionate" might include "caring," "loving" and "kind" while, for another, "Kind" might encompass "compassionate," "loving" and "caring." The idea is not to discover which is "right" from Mr. Webster's or Mr. Roget's point of view, but which resonates most clearly within *you*.

Start to play around with the qualities and actions in a sentence that starts with "I am..." A purpose is short, pithy and to the point. There's usually room for only one or two qualities and an action. "I am a cheerful giver," "I am a joyful explorer," "I am a compassionate friend."

Please consider our grammatical structure as a starting point. "I am a minstrel of God," "I sing the song of life" or "I serve the planet" are outstanding purposes that don't fit the "I am a [quality] [action]" format. Go to the *spirit* of what a purpose is—the *purpose* of a purpose, if you will—and find your purpose there.

After a while of rearranging qualities and actions, something will click. A voice inside will say, "Yes, this is what I've always done, and this is what I'll always be

*Here is the test
to find whether your mission
on earth is finished:
If you're alive, it isn't.*

RICHARD BACH

doing." (This discovery can come with equal parts joy and resignation—joy at seeing that our life has had a direction all along; resignation in noticing it may not be as *glamorous* as we had secretly hoped.)

And that's your purpose.

You might want to place your purpose in a prominent place in your sanctuary—emblazoned on the wall in letters of fiery gold, or, perhaps, on a hand-sewn sampler.

We suggest you not tell your purpose to anyone. That's why we suggested—as a joke, of course—the Peace Corps ruse. (You didn't *really* tell your friends you were joining the Peace Corps, did you? Oh, dear. All right. Well, call them back, and tell them it wasn't really the Peace Corps. It was really the Nobel Selection Committee. Yeah, that's it. The Nobel Selection Committee has been asking a lot of questions about you, and you wanted to have a few comments prepared, should you unexpectedly be invited to Stockholm.)

Keeping your purpose to yourself is not so much *secret* as it is *sacred*. Consider it a beautiful plant. Keep the roots (the essence of the purpose) deep within yourself, and let the world share in its fruits.

Please save your lists (stacks) of qualities and activities. We'll be using them later.

*Perfections of means and
confusion of goals seem
—in my opinion—
to characterize our age.*

ALBERT EINSTEIN

Intention vs. Method

An intention is what we want. Methods are the ways of getting it. An intention is our heart's desire. Methods are the actions, information, things and behaviors we use to get it.

The intention may be "Go to Chicago." The method might be car, train, walking, flying, roller skating, pogo sticking, etc. For each intention, there are many methods.

Unlike our purpose, which is discovered, an intention is chosen. If our purpose is West, our intention can be any destination West of wherever we happen to be. The choice of that destination is ours.

When you ask some people why they're not living their dream, they usually respond with a listing of unavailable methods: not enough money, looks, information, contacts, breaks, etc. All these are just methods. They may sound rational, but they are, in reality, rational lies.

Most people let their methods decide their intentions. This is a fundamental mistake in manifestation. Those who look at what they already *have* before selecting what they *want* are involved in *making do,* not *doing.*

The reason many people feel bored and unfulfilled is that they spend their lives shuffling and reshuffling the methods they already have. This can be like rearranging deck chairs on the Titanic—no matter how well it's done, the result is the same. As someone said, "If you do what you've always done, you'll get what you've always gotten."

When choosing a dream, look to your heart, not to your "reality." That's why it's called a dream. Make that dream your intention. Commit to it. Act upon that commitment. The methods to fulfill that dream will appear.

An intention might be a method to achieve a greater intention, and that greater intention might be a method for obtaining a greater intention still.

*When I was born
I was so surprised
I didn't talk
for a year and a half.*

GRACIE ALLEN

For example, a taxi might be the method to get to the airport, the airport being the intention. The airport might be the method of getting to Chicago, a larger intention. Chicago might be a method of traveling West, which is a larger intention still, all of which fits within the purpose, "I am joyfully traveling West."

We can add new methods to our lives regardless of age, circumstances, situation, or anything else. It simply requires a *willingness* to learn. And learning methods that can radically improve our lives doesn't necessarily take a lot of time.

Imagine the difference between a newborn infant and a two-year-old. An infant cannot walk, talk, coordinate its body, control its bowels, eat solid food, understand language or see very well. By two, the child is well on the way to mastering all these. That's how much learning a human can do in two years.

That same transformational amount of learning can take place in any similar period of time. In fact, as an adult, we can learn even *faster.* All it takes is commitment and willingness.

We'll discuss the techniques of commitment and willingness later. For now, feel free to choose a goal that seems "impossible." Possible and impossible are simply terms to describe how many methods one has available that already fit the goal. In fact, why not choose for yourself the intention to create a perfect intention?

☆

Meanwhile, here is some Good Advice to ponder:

"Never eat anything whose listed ingredients cover more than one-third the package." (Joseph Leonard)

"Have a place for everything and keep the thing somewhere else; this is not a piece of advice, it is merely a custom." (Mark Twain)

The way you activate the seeds of
your creation is by making
choices about the results you
want to create.
When you make a choice,
you mobilize vast human energies
and resources
which otherwise go untapped.
All too often people fail
to focus their choices upon results
and therefore their choices are
ineffective.
If you limit your choices
only to what seems
possible or reasonable,
you disconnect yourself from what
you truly want,
and all that is left
is a compromise.

ROBERT FRITZ

"Write injuries in dust, benefits in marble." (Benjamin Franklin)

"People will accept your ideas much more readily if you tell them Benjamin Franklin said it first." (David H. Comins)

"Let your intentions create your methods and not the other way around." (The authors—although Benjamin Franklin said it first)

"Follow your bliss." (Joseph Campbell)

"After ecstasy, the laundry." (Zen statement.)

Love is but the discovery
of ourselves in others,
and the delight
in the recognition.

ALEXANDER SMITH

Needs vs. Wants

Let's be clear about this—any time we refer to "wants" in this book, we mean *wants,* not *needs*.

Our needs are already fulfilled, and have been fulfilled—consistently—from the time we were born, until this very moment.

We can make this seemingly bold statement, and include you in it, because, if it *weren't* true, you wouldn't be reading this book. In fact, you wouldn't be here at all. When human needs are not fulfilled, death occurs. Period.

Needs are food, shelter, clothing, air, water and protection. (Even this may be a long list: "shelter," "clothing" and "protection" cover pretty much the same ground—keeping the elements and the elephants at bay.) Everything else we *think* we need is a want.

The rule of thumb: if you can live without it for even a short period of time, it's a want. We didn't say *happily* live without it, or *comfortably* live without it—just *live* without it, as in *exist*.

"Not love?" some might protest. Whoever or whatever is providing you with food, clothing, shelter, air, water and protection loves you beyond measure. Romantic love ("I love you. Sigh." "I love you, too. Sigh.") is all very nice—but it's a want, not a need.

We get into trouble when we call a want a need—it begins to corrupt our integrity. When we say we *need* something, the body goes into red alert. Need? That's like food, water, air! The body—the whole being, in fact—uses all its resources to meet the need *right away*. After too many false alarms, it becomes the story of the little boy who cried "Wolf!" once too often. Eventually, our urgent plea of "I need!" is ignored.

Meanwhile, a part of us is patiently waiting to help us fulfill our *wants*. The simple statement, "I want...," committed to and acted upon, can move mountains. When we

This above all:
to thine own self be true,
And it must follow,
as the night the day,
Thou canst not then be false
to any man.

SHAKESPEARE

call our wants "needs," however, a part of us says, "OK, let's just see how much you *really* need this."

As a poet once put it, "My needs destroy the paths by which those needs could be fulfilled."

Yes, we do need, but those needs are entirely physical. Emotionally, we are whole and complete just as we are (although we may not *realize* that fully as yet).

Saying we need something outside ourselves in order to have a positive feeling within (joy, happiness, love) implies that we are somehow *lacking*. This is simply not the case. In this sense, saying "I need..." is an affirmation of personal deficiency—even if it is followed by very nice words.

Take, for example, "I need to give my love to others." The giving of one's love to others is all very nice, but the inherent lack in the "I need..." part of the sentence pollutes the whole thing. "I want to give my love to others" is so much, well, less desperate, and somehow, um, *nicer.*

It's fine to want something *a whole lot*. That's part of the process of manifestation. The next section of this book, in fact, is about becoming more passionate about our dream. When we start calling a want a need, however, we step over the line from being *passionate* to being impoverished.

What we *need* is always supplied to us, and always will be, until the day we die. Let us be grateful for that. And let's pursue our wants and desires from this platform of fulfillment and gratitude.

*We forfeit three-fourths of
ourselves to be like other people.*

ARTHUR SCHOPENHAUER

1788-1860

Selfish vs. Selfing

Yes, we're going to coin a word here. (What would a self-help book be without a coined word or two?) The word we're going to coin is *selfing*.

Selfing means doing for one's Self, in the larger sense of Self, as in True Self, or "To thine own self be true." It means fulfilling the dreams, goals and aspirations inherent within us. It means living our life "on purpose."

Selfish, on the other hand, is the petty, endlessly greedy gathering of stuff (houses, cars, boats, clothes), stuff (husbands, wives, children, lovers), and more stuff (power, fame, money, sex). It's the relentless pursuit of glamour at all costs. It's worshipping the god of other people's opinion.

Selfing is knowing what you want—what *you* want, not what you *should* want because others *say* you should want it—and moving toward it. Others may call you selfish, but you know that you are selfing—"being yourself."

As Ralph Waldo Trine explained, "There are many who are living far below their possibilities because they are continually handing over their individualities to others. Do you want to be a power in the world? Then be yourself. Be true to the highest within your soul and then allow yourself to be governed by no customs or conventionalities or arbitrary man-made rules that are not founded on principle."

Those who do fulfill their dreams, *naturally* share that fulfillment with all those around them. Inviting others to enjoy the advantages of the goal is inherent in the process of realizing a dream; it's an organic part of the process.

Someone studying to be a doctor may spend all her time, energy and resources on learning. For several years, she may appear to others to be "selfish." She will, however, spend the remainder of her lifetime applying what she has learned during this "selfish" period to benefit others. Was it truly selfish after all?

*The only man
who is really free
is the one who can turn down
an invitation to dinner
without giving an excuse.*

JULES RENARD

Selfing is putting yourself first in the abundance of now.

George Bernard Shaw explained the difference between selfing and selfish when he wrote, "This is the true joy in life, the being used for a purpose recognized by yourself as a mighty one; the being thoroughly worn out before you are thrown on the scrap heap; the being a force of nature instead of a feverish selfish little clod of ailments and grievances complaining that the world will not devote itself to making you happy."

Shaw's first use of "self" ("...a purpose recognized by yourself as a mighty one...") would be the large Self, his second use ("...a feverish selfish little clod...") would be the petty self.

In moving toward your goal, it may be necessary to use all your available resources toward the fulfillment of that goal. That's to be expected, and that's selfing. Others (especially those who have some of your resources—such as time and attention—taken from them) may call you selfish. The question is, "What's more important—your goal, or others' opinions of your goal?"

It's amazing how many people—through their actions—answer the latter.

*When the eagles are silent
the parrots begin to jabber.*

SIR WINSTON CHURCHILL

You Can Have Anything You Want, But You Can't Have Everything You Want

Here it is, the chapter that was foretold to you so many times. The phrase "you can have anything you want, but you can't have everything you want" sums up this whole section of the book.

You can have anything you want: No dream is too big to achieve. If *one other* person has achieved it, you can be the second. If *no other* person has achieved it, you can be the first. Dream big, dear reader, dream big.

But you can't have everything you want: We live in a finite world for a finite period of time, but with an infinite imagination. Our imagination can create more wants than a computer can generate random numbers. We're not going to have time for all the wants we want.

There are those who say, "I want it all!" We wonder, if they ever got it all, where would they put it? When would they find the time to use it all, or even the time to *learn* how to use it all? One begins to get images from *Citizen Kane*—warehouse after warehouse stuffed with art treasures, purchased but never uncrated.

In fact, we *can't* "have it all"—there's simply not enough time. To make "having it all" a goal is not realistic. Long before we get "it all" we run out of time, energy and resources. Maybe that's why people who "want it all" often look so *tired.*

More often, however, we encounter people who don't want enough. Oh, they may want *enough* in the sense of a little here and a little there and all the littles add up to "enough." Unfortunately, many of those littles aren't what they *really want*—they're littles they think they *should* want because somebody said they should want them. If they had their heart's desire—the Big Want—they would gladly "sacrifice" most of the little littles.

We have only so much time and so much energy and so many resources, and we're going to spend them on

*People are always blaming
their circumstances
for what they are.
I don't believe
in circumstances.
The people who get on
in this world are the people
who get up and look for the
circumstances they want,
and, if they can't find them,
make them.*

GEORGE BERNARD SHAW

1893

something. The tragedy in most people's lives is that they spend that time, energy and resources *doing something other than their heart's desire.*

We are, of course, never given more time. We all have 24 hours each day. We're going to spend that time doing *something*. Why not spend it pursuing our dreams? Energy and resources come in, as needed, to fulfill the purpose.

It's when we have *too many* purposes ("I want to visit Los Angeles, New York, Chicago and Denver, all in one day"), or purposes that *conflict* with each other (try starting from Kansas and going to New York *and* Los Angeles simultaneously), that we run up against "you can't have *everything* you want."

Yes, we are worthy of visiting *any* of those cities, but not *all* of them at once. Most people, however, rather than *choosing* one, just give up and stay in Kansas. "I can't have anything I want," they sigh.

They *can* have anything they want, but they *can't* have everything they want. There is more to life than Kansas. The key is choosing what we want most (our heart's desire), letting go of everything else we want (for now), and moving (mentally, emotionally and physically) toward our goal.

The choosing, letting go and moving is what we're going to look at next. It is, in fact, the essence of how to DO IT!

If someone says "can't,"
that shows you what to do.

JOHN CAGE

The Biggest Lie in Choosing

The biggest lie in choosing is, "I can't."

That is simply not true.

We *can* do anything we want. If we *don't* do something, it is because we have committed our time, energy and resources somewhere else.

The next time you hear yourself saying, to another—and especially to yourself—"I can't," take a deep breath and say instead, "My resources are otherwise engaged."

Because that's the truth.

Lots of folks confuse bad management with destiny.

KIN HUBBARD

Life's Four Basic Areas of Activity

When choosing a dream to follow, it's good to consider the four basic areas in which people live. They are

- Marriage/Family
- Career/Professional
- Social/Political
- Religious/Spiritual

Naturally, in the course of a lifetime, people tend to spend some time in each. Looking back, however, most people can say, "Yes, I gave the majority of my time and attention to _____" and mention one of the categories. Sometimes, it's the area they *wanted* to spend most of their time in. Other times, they spent their life in an area other than the one closest to their heart.

In choosing *now* which area you feel most drawn to, you can either (A) spend more time in that area, or (B) realize that the draw you feel ("I really want to do this, but I think I *should* do that") is from programming other than your own. Now is a good time to reprogram yourself so that the goals you follow are your own.

Here's where the "I want it all" syndrome comes in. We somehow think we're *entitled* to a *significant* goal from *each* of the four categories. All at once. Sorry. We haven't seen it. You can have *any* category you want, but you can't have *every* category you want.

It's easier to face this hard reality of life sooner than later. (Some people are reading this book because the hard reality came knocking on their door...or repossessed the house, or filed divorce proceedings, or got them fired, or, or, or.)

You *can* spend equal amounts of time in each category, but, if you do, don't expect to go very far in any of them. You will live "a balanced life." People will remark to you, "My, what a balanced life you live."

The heights by great men
reached and kept
Were not attained
by sudden flight,
But they, while their
companions slept,
Were toiling upward
in the night.

HENRY WADSWORTH LONGFELLOW

If, in imagining this, a part of you says, "I don't want a balanced life! I want to be a rock star!" (Career/Professional) or "All I care about is my family!" (Marriage/Family) or "What difference does a balanced life make if we can't breathe the air?" (Social/Political) or "This world is but the shadowlands; the greater world is beyond!" (Religious/Spiritual), then perhaps you're not looking for the balanced life after all.

The narrower your goal—and the more fully you supply that goal with all your time, energy and resources—the farther you'll go and the faster you'll get there. Think of a rocket. All the energy is pinpointed in one direction, and it can zoom off to distant planets.

The downside of rocket travel? You can't bring your house *and* your family *and* report for work on time *and* save the whales *and* take all your religious and spiritual books *and*...etc. Very little fits in the capsule of a rocket. If, however, seeing the moon close-up and in-person is your heart's desire, letting go of all but that "very little" is the price you must pay.

"All right. I'll settle for *pictures* of the moon."

Much less investment is required for that. You can even have a *video* of the moon. In color. Let go, however, of the dream of seeing the moon in-person and close-up. It will free-up energy you can put toward the dream you *do* choose to achieve.

In the next four chapters, we'll take a look at each of the four basic areas of activity. Along the way, we'll dispel a few of the myths that have grown around each. These are, for the most part, things that anyone who's done them will tell you. We thought you might want to know before spending, oh, twenty years finding out.

Before discussing the four areas, let us first mention a concept called The Mirror.

The mirror concept says that all life is a mirror, and by looking into the mirror of life, we can learn a great deal about ourselves. The mirror concept asks, "What if everything you like in people and things around you is

The only service
a friend can really render
is to keep up your courage by
holding up to you a mirror
in which you can see
a noble image of yourself.

GEORGE BERNARD SHAW

really reflecting back to you something you like about yourself?" If you admire people who are kind, for example, they are reflecting back to you the kindness within yourself.

On the other hand, the mirror also reflects back what we don't like about ourselves. When we dislike someone for being selfish, perhaps there's a selfishness within ourselves that we don't like.

The mirror works just as well with things as with people. In fact, it's sometimes easier to see that we're projecting our feelings about ourselves onto something else when the object is inanimate. If we're moved by the grandeur of the sky, it's obvious that the grandeur is our projection. The sky is the sky. No grandeur there, other than the grandeur we put there.

Using the mirror concept, we can use everything in life to teach us more about ourselves. Each area of life acts as a magnifying mirror to one aspect or another of ourselves. The area of ourselves we find most intriguing—the one we would most like to explore—is often the one we gravitate toward when choosing an area of life with which to become involved.

*If you want to sacrifice
the admiration of many men
for the criticism of one,
go ahead, get married.*

KATHERINE HEPBURN

Marriage and Family

The myths about marriage and family are omnipresent in our culture. The myths are perpetrated in almost every movie, TV show, song, magazine, book, billboard and advertisement.

The mythical scene goes something like this: You are trudging along in life—lonely, but coping. Some Enchanted Evening (across a crowded room) you meet The Perfect Stranger (as opposed to a total stranger). Fade in music. Fade out loneliness. You are lifted to the pinnacle of bliss, where you and Prince Charming or Cinderella live happily ever after.

This is the most popular version of the larger, underlying myth that says things and people outside ourselves can make us happy. ("You made me love you, I didn't want to do it...")

In fact, *we* make us happy. ("If you are lonely when you are alone," cautioned Jean-Paul Sartre, "you are in bad company.") The joy we see in others is a reflection of the joy in ourselves. We feel uncomfortable, however, giving ourselves credit for our own joy. It's easier to say, "You're wonderful, and I'm so happy you're with me," than to say, "I'm wonderful, and I'm so happy to be me." It may be easier to *say*, but it's not (A) honest, and (B) easy to live.

It's not easy to live because, if we feel happiness only when that other person is around, then we have to keep that other person around in order to be happy. If that person happens to be lost in the same illusion, that's called "being in love," and everything is hunky dory—for a while. (As Cher observed, "The trouble with some women is that they get all excited about nothing—and then marry him.")

Eventually, no matter how hard we keep up the facade, one or the other will peek behind it and see The Dark Side, which is not at all lovable. "He loved me absolutely," wrote Frieda (Mrs. D. H.) Lawrence, "that's why he hates me absolutely."

Seldom or never does a marriage develop into an individual relationship smoothly and without crisis. There is no birth of consciousness without pain.

C. G. JUNG

The Dark Side is, of course, only something we see in another that we don't like about ourselves, and, again, are not honest enough to admit. If A sees B's Dark Side, but B fails to see A's Dark Side, it's Dump City. A cries, "Free Again!" and B sings a medley of torch songs. If both see it at once, the perfect lovers become the perfect enemies.

Are we being harsh on love and marriage? Look at the statistics. In the United States, half the marriages end in divorce within five years. *Half!* ("In Hollywood all the marriages are happy," Shelley Winters observed. "It's trying to live together afterwards that causes all the problems.")

Remember, these are the couples who stood before God, friends and in-laws, *swearing* to love one another till death did them part. Imagine how many others, who thought they were in love forever, never made it to the altar. ("My boyfriend and I broke up," Rita Rudner explained, "He wanted to get married and I didn't want him to.")

Which brings us to children. Children are a 24-hour-a-day commitment, for a minimum of eighteen years—probably longer. With children, you can learn something very important: how to give for the sheer joy of giving. If you give to children with any hope of return, you're inviting misery all around. ("Before I was married I had three theories about raising children," John Wilmot, the Earl of Rochester, wrote. "Now I have three children and no theories.")

In fact, that's one of the primary lessons one learns—not just from children but from intimate relationships of all kinds—how to give.

The myth is that marriage is for *receiving*. It's not. It's for giving. ("Marriage is not merely sharing the fettucini," Calvin Trillin explained, "but sharing the burden of finding the fettucini restaurant in the first place.")

Don't take our word for it. Ask anyone who's been in a successful relationship for, oh, at least two years. They'll almost certainly describe themselves as *giving*, with no thought of return. If they go on and on about how much fun it was to *receive*, you're probably talking to Zsa Zsa Gabor.

*I have known more men
destroyed by the desire
to have wife and child and
to keep them in comfort
than I have seen destroyed by
drink and harlots.*

WILLIAM BUTLER YEATS

(Zsa Zsa was once on a call-in radio show. The caller asked, "I want to break up with a man, but he's been so nice to me. He gave me a car, a diamond necklace, a mink stole, beautiful gowns, a stove, expensive perfumes—what should I do?" Without having to think, Zsa Zsa said, "Give him back the stove.")

Another cultural myth is that we are somehow *incomplete* if we do not reproduce. This may have had some validity when being fruitful and multiplying was necessary for a species or tribe to continue. Today, however, one of the great problems in the world is overpopulation. Let those who really *want* to reproduce reproduce (and that includes providing the 18-year environment in which the reproductions can grow into functioning, creative, healthy humans). Those who want to leave their legacy in another way can feel free to do so.

Another value of relationship is learning about *ourselves*—the good, the bad, the beautiful and the ugly. Marriage is like a dinner with desert first. The falling in love portion shows us the beauty within us. Everything else shows us everything else. It's a package deal. When The Dark Side presents itself and says, "I'm in you, too. Learn to love and accept me in yourself," many people panic.

"Wait a minute. This isn't part of the contract."

"Yes it is. For better or for worse. This is worse."

"This is *the worst*. Where's the lovey-dovey stuff?"

"Maybe that bird will return when you learn to love this one."

"I have to learn to love it?"

"You only *have to* learn to *accept* it. Loving it, however, feels better."

People seldom want to face the Dark Side of themselves. Instead, they (choose one or more):

1. Deny it's a mirror and pretend it's the other person. (One must be careful not to strike out too severely

*As to marriage or celibacy, let a man
take which course he will—
he will be sure to repent it.*

SOCRATES

*For one human being to love another:
that is perhaps the most difficult of all
our tasks, the ultimate, the last test and
proof, the work for which all other
work is but preparation.*

RAINER MARIA RILKE

at a mirror, for, as we all know, if you break a mirror, it's seven years bad luck—perhaps in jail.)

2. Pretend *really hard* that everything is all right, and "play house." ("Welcome to *At Home with the Ostrich Family*. Here's mother, Heroic Pretender; and father, General Denial. Here are their children, Make Believe, Gloss Over and Feign Affection. Don't they look *happy?* The Ostrich Family!")

3. See that the reflected Dark Side they see in the mirror is true about themselves and hate themselves even more.

4. Run!

For those looking for an intensive workshop in self-discovery, self-acceptance, and the perfect place to learn The Joy of Giving, Marriage/Family is an area of life to consider.

(If you thought we were perhaps too hard on marital bliss, let's close with a romantic thought from Britt Ekland: "I know a lot of people didn't expect our relationship to last —but we just celebrated our two months anniversary.")

*I don't have anything against work.
I just figure, why deprive somebody
who really loves it?*

DOBIE GILLIS

*NAPOLEON SOLO: Are you free?
ILLYA KURAKIN: No man is free who has
to work for a living. But I am available.*

THE MAN FROM U.N.C.L.E.

Career and Professional

Did you ever hear parents placing a curse upon their child? "Someday, something's going to straighten you out!" That's what a career is—The Great Straightener.

Next to gravity, there's very little as constant as the business world—it will drag you down if you slip too often, or hurl you to the moon if you understand how to use it. (Most of the energy used in traveling to the moon and back was the gravitational pull of the moon and Earth.) Wernher von Braun found the business side of putting a man on the moon more difficult than the functional side. "We can lick gravity," he said, "but sometimes the paperwork is overwhelming."

A *job* is what you have when you want to take money to some other area of life in order to buy the necessities of life. Someone whose primary focus is marriage, for example, leaves the marriage only long enough to make enough money to support the marriage—baby needs a new pair of shoes, and all that. That's a job.

(Not that staying home and working isn't a job. To illuminate, here's Roseanne Barr: "As a housewife, I feel that if the kids are still alive when my husband gets home from work, then hey, I've done my job. When Sears comes out with a riding vacuum cleaner, then I'll clean the house." One could follow Quentin Crisp's advice, "There is no need to do any housework at all. After the first four years the dirt doesn't get any worse. It's simply a question of not losing your *nerve*.")

A *career* or *profession* is when the thing you love doing most is what you also get paid for doing, so you can do it all the time. As Noel Coward said, "Work is much more fun than fun." Or, as Richard Bach remarked, "The more I want to get something done, the less I call it work."

"But I am an artist," some may say. "I only want to create." If you plan to get paid for creating, then you're in business. "But someone will discover me and take care of all that." Right, and if you have nothing to wear to the

*Drive thy business,
or it will drive thee.*

BENJAMIN FRANKLIN

ball, your fairy godmother will supervise the mice and the birds in making you a gown.

The days of being "discovered" in the arts went out with Diaghelev and Lana Turner. Artists—and that includes actors, singers, writers, dancers, musicians, painters, and so on—must become their own supporters, must champion their own cause. To succeed, they must become patron and protegee, all in one. In other words, if you're a creative person, you must create your own creative outlet. And that means being in business.

(In 1988, twenty publishers turned down our first book, *You Can't Afford the Luxury of a Negative Thought,* so we published it ourselves. We then published *LIFE 101* ourselves, and this one, too, because we realized there's a lot more to getting a book into our readers' hands than merely writing it.)

The secret of success in a career? Same as success in any other area. As John Moores explained, "Work seven days a week and nothing can stop you." Not only is it hard work, it's hard, *challenging* work. "If you have a job without aggravations," Malcolm Forbes pointed out, "you don't have a job."

One must, however, not just work *hard.* One must work *smart.* As the saying goes, the efficient person gets the job done *right;* the effective person gets the right job done. "The really idle man gets nowhere," Sir Heneage Ogilvie observed. "The perpetually busy man does not get much further."

Of course, a career is not for everyone. Lily Tomlin said, "The trouble with the rat race is that even if you win, you're still a rat."

And, yes, in addition to long hours and hard work, each career has its Dark Side. "The price one pays for pursuing any profession or calling," James Baldwin explained, "is an intimate knowledge of its ugly side."

When one peeks through the glamour, one sees what's real, and one may not like it. As Fred Allen said, "When you get through all the phony tinsel of Hollywood, you

*It is your work in life that is
the ultimate seduction.*

PABLO PICASSO

find the genuine tinsel underneath." David Sarnoff remarked, "Competition brings out the best in products, and the worst in people."

One *especially* may not like it when one remembers the mirror—the things we don't like about our career are also what we don't like about ourselves. Is your career insincere? Dishonest? Heartless? Gulp. Behold, the mirror.

If one is willing to see a career as a great, big mirror (career and mirror—they even rhyme, if you pronounce them with a vague, Southern accent), there's a lot to learn —things most people *don't* want to learn about themselves.

Rather than looking in either the relationship or career mirrors, some spend time looking in one until it becomes uncomfortable, then run off to look in the other. Back and forth, eternally.

The career vs. marriage struggle has been going on since the caveperson who invented the first wheel decided to open *Wheels R Us.*

One side of the discussion is expressed by George Jean Nathan: "Marriage is based on the theory that when a man discovers a brand of beer exactly to his taste he should at once throw up his job and go to work in a brewery."

Representing the other side of the argument, we present Bertrand Russell: "One of the symptoms of an approaching nervous breakdown is the belief that one's work is terribly important."

"Can't I have both a career and a marriage?" Well, some can. And some can juggle seven balls while eating a tuna fish sandwich.

What happens at the end of a long, successful career? You'll be glad you chose career over everything else, brimming with pride over all you've accomplished, right?

Well...

T. S. Eliot, poet, Nobel Laureate—but better known as the lyricist for *Cats,* heaven help his memory—wrote, "As things are, and as fundamentally they must always be, poetry is not a career, but a mug's game. No honest poet

*The easiest kind of
relationship for me
is with ten thousand people.
The hardest is with one.*

JOAN BAEZ

can ever feel quite sure of the permanent value of what he has written: he may have wasted his time and messed up his life for nothing."

And Sir Thomas More, after fifteen years of practicing law, wrote in his view of an ideal future, *Utopia,* "They have no lawyers among them, for they consider them as a sort of people whose profession it is to disguise matters."

Or, as Robert Frost put it, "By working faithfully eight hours a day, you may eventually get to be a boss and work twelve hours a day."

To laugh often and much;
to win the respect of intelligent
people and the affection of
children; to earn the appreciation
of honest critics and endure the
betrayal of false friends;
to appreciate beauty;
to find the best in others;
to leave the world a bit better,
whether by a healthy child,
a garden patch or a
redeemed social condition;
to know even one life has
breathed easier
because you have lived.
This is to have succeeded.

EMERSON

Social and Political

If the sentence, "I love humanity, it's people I can't stand," fits you, perhaps you should consider a life of social change and political action.

"The only thing necessary for the triumph of evil," Edmund Burke wrote two hundred years ago, "is for good men to do nothing." The world has any number of good people right now, with the dream to make changes for the better deep in their hearts. The problem is not that they're doing *nothing*, the problem is that they're doing *something else*.

People who are naturally drawn toward social action or politics are often repelled by its name. "Ninety percent of the politicians give the other ten percent a bad reputation," Henry Kissinger said. Here is an area of activity where the *reputation* is worse than the *reality*—a sort of reverse glamour.

"I used to say that politics was the second oldest profession," said Ronald Reagan in 1979, "and I have come to know that it bears a gross similarity to the first." The following year, however, he won the presidency.

"Nobody could sleep with Dick," Pat Nixon revealed. "He wakes up during the night, switches on the lights, speaks into his tape recorder, or takes notes—it's impossible."

John Updike had this explanation for the inconsistency of our leaders: "A leader is one who, out of madness or goodness, volunteers to take upon himself the woe of the people. There are few men so foolish, hence the erratic quality of leadership in the world."

And yet, with all the bad things written about it, some do have good words for and about the art of politics.

"True leadership must be for the benefit of the followers," wrote Robert Townsend in *Up the Organization,* "not the enrichment of the leaders." Townsend was speaking of the business world, but it applies to the political world just as well.

*A cardinal rule of politics—
never get caught in bed with a
live man or a dead woman.*

J.R. EWING

You may not always be popular, even among those you are helping. Harry Truman asked, "How far would Moses have gone if he had taken a poll in Egypt?"

"Public life is regarded as the crown of a career, and to young men it is the worthiest ambition," said John Buchan. "Politics is still the greatest and the most honorable adventure."

"Politics," Gore Vidal wrote, with his own enticing twist on Buchan, "is the grim jockeying for position, the ceaseless trading, the deliberate use of words not for communication but to screen intention. In short, a splendidly exciting game for those who play it."

"If you're going to play the game properly," cautioned Barbara Jordan, "you'd better know every rule."

The great social causes that capture the hearts of men and women do not necessarily involve politics. They do, however, involve courage, sacrifice, commitment, and selfless giving—sort of the worst of marriage and career combined.

There are, however, inner benefits. "The great use of life is to spend it for something that will outlast it," William James said, in words that outlasted him.

And let's make no mistake about it: we make social changes because, over time, it makes *us* feel better. We may not appreciate the day-to-day tilting at windmills, but we prefer that to, day-by-day, observing a condition we know we could somehow make better, get worse.

People often think a social problem is too great, and they are too small. We suggest: If drawn to do it, do it. "What one has to do," Eleanor Roosevelt pointed out, "usually can be done."

The reward is the joy of giving, the satisfaction of following your heart's desire, and, perhaps, someone will say of you what Clare Boothe Luce said of Eleanor Roosevelt, "No woman has ever so comforted the distressed—or distressed the comfortable."

*I know God will not give me
anything I can't handle.
I just wish that He didn't
trust me so much.*

MOTHER TERESA

Religious and Spiritual

Here we co-authors tread softly. In *LIFE 101,* we put all the religious and spiritual beliefs—from Anglicanism to agnosticism to atheism to Catholicism—in an area we called The Gap.

The contents of anyone's Gap is between the person and the contents of his or her Gap. We don't get involved with the Gap in these books because the tools we discuss work regardless of what's in anyone's Gap, just as a cookbook or car repair manual works for the Baptist and the Buddhist alike.

In discussing the areas of life's activity, however, we must touch upon an area certain people are strongly drawn to—religion and spirit.

What can we say, other than—if this is your heart's desire, follow it.

There is an interesting ambivalence to religion and spirituality in our culture. On one hand, if people have no beliefs, they are thought odd. On the other hand, if they devote all their time to the understanding and worship of God, they, too, are thought odd.

As with politics, people may hesitate pursuing Spirit full time because religion has been so, well, shall we say (tap, tap, tap) has made God to look, uh, um (tap, tap, tap—that's us co-authors tap dancing while arriving at a diplomatic, nonjudgemental way of saying this), perhaps some people's behavior has not cast The Deity in the best possible light.

For example, the chief executive of a *very* popular soft drink company said, "It's a religion as well as a business." (By the way, do you know that the taste of cola is a combination of three familiar flavors? Which Three? If you want to guess, we'll wait for a bit before telling you.)

Others seem to use God as some great bellhop in the sky—"give me this, send me that, take this away"—a little, um, uh, silly. Dorothy Parker parodied these people

I am ready to meet my Maker.
Whether my Maker is prepared for the
ordeal of meeting me is another matter.

WINSTON CHURCHILL

What's a cult?
It just means not enough
people to make a minority.

ROBERT ALTMAN

when she wrote, "Oh God, in the name of Thine only beloved Son, Jesus Christ, Our Lord, let him phone me *now*."

All of this—and we haven't even *mentioned* televangelists and their traumas—may have made traditional religion seem a little strange, even to those who feel a calling. Our advice: follow your heart.

Some want to explore less traditional forms of contacting the Divine, but don't because all that seems weird, too. All we can say is that every major religion was, at one time, a small group of people surrounded by a culture that thought them awfully bizarre. As Tom Wolfe pointed out, "A cult is a religion with no political power." Again, follow your heart—but, as always, don't forget your head.

Of course, there are those who think they *should* spend all their time worshipping God because, after all, God is God and isn't that what we're *supposed* to do? And, even though these people are off pursuing a goal in another area of life, they feel *guilty* for not *praying* more—as though God were an overanxious mother who hasn't had a phone call in a month. (Although, if that is your image of God, far be it from us to de-Deify you.) Might we suggest to these people that they let their good works in whatever field they choose glorify God? (Cola, by the way, is made up of these three flavors: citrus [lemon or lime], vanilla and cinnamon.)

And for those who are feeling the Ultimate Unworthiness—not worthy to serve God—we offer you this from Phyllis McGinley: "The wonderful thing about saints is that they were human. They lost their tempers, scolded God, were egotistical or testy or impatient in their turns, made mistakes and regretted them. Still they went on doggedly blundering toward heaven."

*I can think of nothing
less pleasurable than a life
devoted to pleasure.*

JOHN D. ROCKEFELLER, JR.

Let's Not Forget Fun and Recreation

We're not sure whether all work and no play made Jack a dull boy, or whether Jack was a dull boy to begin with, so, dullard that he was, he worked too much. Either way, fun and recreation are a necessary part of an undull life.

When we say *recreation,* we mean it in the lighter sense of recreation (tennis, boating, going to the movies), as well as in the deeper sense—*re-creation.* What do you do to recreate yourself? This might include meditation, retreats *(re-treats),* prayer, spiritual work, rest, pilgrimages, massage, silent time—whatever activities recharge your batteries in a deep and powerful way.

We didn't include Fun/Recreation in the other areas of life because we assume this is an area people will want to enjoy no matter what other area of life they choose. To use the battery analogy, Fun/Recreation charges the batteries; Marriage/Family, Career/Professional, Social/Political, and Religious/Spiritual are the ways in which the batteries are used.

It's important to realize, however, that the endless pursuit of fun and recreation *in and of themselves* is not very fulfilling. In fact, it's something of a curse. When one pursues pleasure *all the time,* the pursuit of pleasure becomes work—it's a job. If pleasure is one's job, then where does one go to recharge the batteries for more work? The pleasure *is* the work. Hence, perhaps, the old saying about not mixing business with pleasure.

Fun and recreation form a stable base for fulfilling one's dreams—they're just not a very good dream all by themselves.

A Code of Honor—
Never approach a friend's
girlfriend or wife with
mischief as your goal.
There are just too many
women in the world
to justify that sort of
dishonorable behavior.
Unless she's <u>really</u> attractive.

BRUCE JAY FRIEDMAN

Relationships

Please don't think from the tone of the last few chapters that the only way to pursue a dream other than marriage and family is to become a hermit. Far from it.

Relationships are essential to the pursuit of almost any goal. In successfully achieving a goal, however, it is important to understand the different *types* of relationships that are available. When you do, you can see which types of relationships can best help you pursue your dream.

Before exploring the types of relationships humans tend to have, here are two essential points about relationships generally. First, all relationships are with yourself—and sometimes they involve other people. Second, the most important relationship in your life—the one you'll have, like it or not, until the day you die—is with yourself.

That said, let's look at the various types of human relationships.

Recreational Relationships: These are the people we enjoy being with simply because we enjoy being with them. *What* we do together is not as important as *that we are* together.

These are the people we generally call "friends." We love them in a nonpossessive sense. "Love without attachment is light," wrote Norman O. Brown. We see people in recreational relationships for what they are. "We don't love qualities," Jacques Maritain explained, "we love a person; sometimes by reason of their defects as well as their qualities."

Again, the word "recreational" should not be misread as "always superficial." These can be some of the most re-creative and nurturing relationships in our lives.

Among the many things that *can* (although usually doesn't) take place in a recreational relationship is sex. This is fine, as long as neither person looks upon the other as "the one and only."

*The consuming desire of most
human beings is deliberately
to plant their whole life in the
hands of some other person.
I would describe this method
of searching for happiness
as immature.
Development of character
consists solely in moving
toward self-sufficiency.*

QUENTIN CRISP

Romantic Relationships: Here, sex—or sexual desire—combines with a feeling of, "you are the only one for me," and "if you don't love me, I'm miserable and worthless." We don't have to like—or even *know*—the "love object." Some say ignorance is a *prerequisite* for romantic love. "Of course it is possible to love a human being," wrote Charles Bukowski, "if you don't know them too well."

Romantic love is the most popularized of all relationships. Just about every movie, TV show, novel and popular song features romantic interaction. It's called the "love interest." It seemingly must be worked into every plot, no matter how silly or tortured.

Why? Because romantic love is a primary cultural myth of our time. As George Lucas explained to Steven Spielberg (these are the two who *somehow* squeezed a "love interest" into all of those Indiana Jones movies), "If the boy and girl walk off in the sunset hand-in-hand in the last scene, it adds ten million to the box office."

We call romantic love ("If only you could find the right person to love, you would live happily ever after") a myth because no other human endeavor has failed so miserably, so often—yet continues to have such "good press."

Not everyone, of course, believes "the press." "I can understand companionship," said Gore Vidal, "I can understand purchased sex in the afternoon. I cannot understand the love affair." Margaret Anderson explained it this way, "In real love you want the other person's good. In romantic love you want the other person."

Some people "fall in love" rather than deal with the guilt often associated with sex. "If we love each other, sex is OK," the logic goes. "Love is the drug," wrote Germaine Greer, "which makes sexuality palatable in popular mythology."

Romantic love is a primary distraction to the pursuit of *any* goal, *including* Marriage/Family. We should say *especially* Marriage/Family. The illusion of "falling in love" can blind one to the suitability of a partner for a venture

*Basically my wife
was immature. I'd be at home
in the bath and she'd come in
and sink my boats.*

WOODY ALLEN

as delicate, intricate, and important as getting married and raising children. (Or even getting married and raising *orchids.)*

"Many a man has fallen in love with a girl," Maurice Chevalier observed, "in light so dim he would not have chosen a suit by it." And, many a person has chosen a mate in a light of reason dimmer than that.

In addition, the *lack* of romantic love is hardly sufficient reason to eliminate another otherwise-qualified candidate from a list of potential spouses—and yet it's done all the time. People say, "They'd be a wonderful husband/wife, but I don't really *love* them." You might as well use romantic love as a criteria for going into business, or any other significant partnership.

It is this blindness, as much as anything else, that accounts for the many failures in the pursuit of a successful marriage. If you think running a house and raising children *isn't* a business, you've never run a house and raised children.

"Love is an ideal thing," said Goethe, "marriage is a real thing. A confusion of the real with the ideal never goes unpunished."

Contractual Relationships: In a contractual relationship, something is exchanged for something else. The "something" could be anything—a product, a service, an experience. Usually the culturally agreed upon *symbol* for energy—money—is involved in the transaction.

When we pay someone for something, or to do something for us, that is a contractual relationship. When somebody pays us for something, or to do something for them, that, too, is a contractual relationship. It could be as basic as buying a box of cough drops at the store (even such a simple transaction involves entering into a contract), or as elaborate as a fifty-year partnership—including marriage.

In a contractual relationship, we are "in relationship" primarily because of the exchange. We can enjoy each

Since I was twenty-four there never was any vagueness in my plans or ideas as to what God's work was for me.

FLORENCE NIGHTINGALE

other's company or not. If so, that's an extra plus. If not, too bad—we're in it for something else.

"Almost all of our relationships begin," explained W. H. Auden, "and most of them continue as forms of mutual exploitation, a mental or physical barter, to be terminated when one or both parties run out of goods."

Common-Goal Relationships: Here people share a common goal, and that goal is the primary reason they relate. This is often the source of work-based relationships. The common goal may be a company goal, a personal goal fulfilled by the company, or, simply, as Sir Noel Coward put it, "your pay packet at the end of the week."

It might be a service goal—relating to fellow Red Cross volunteers, for example. It might be a religious or spiritual goal—the people you know in church, or who pursue the same spiritual dreams as you.

The marriages that continue "for the sake of the children" are also examples of common-goal relationships— the raising of the children being the common goal. "The value of marriage," said Peter De Vries, "is not that adults produce children, but that children produce adults."

Power-Point Relationships: This is a specific form of common-goal relationships. Here one person (or team of people) becomes the "power point." A group feeds its energy (power) to the power-point person, and through this power point, the entire group can fulfill its common goal.

An example is the Olympic athlete training for an event. Power from many people is given to this one person. The "power" may be in the form of information, encouragement, money, time—anything the athlete needs to meet the goal. A trainer, coach, corporate sponsor, masseur, doctor, nutritionist—and many others—channel their power (in the form of individual specialties) to the athlete. They all have the same goal—winning the event—and send power to a single point so that the goal can be fulfilled.

Think of the point-person as the point of the arrow. The point is the portion of the arrow that "does the work,"

If the point is sharp,
and the arrow is swift,
it can pierce through the dust
no matter how thick.

BOB DYLAN

but the shaft, feathers, bow and archer are equally as important to hitting the target.

The point person never needs to *return* any of this energy to those giving it. The point person need only do his or her best in the event—the common goal. In so doing—win or lose—the investment of power is "paid back."

In addition to sports, power-point relationships are often seen in politics, the arts, spiritual groups, and, less frequently, in business and marriage. In a marriage, it can work as long as it is understood that partner A's success is the goal of both partner A and partner B—and that partner A's success *in and of itself* is sufficient for partner B. If partner B wants something more from partner A or partner A's success, then it's a contract or common-goal relationship.

☆

In relationships—as in all things—there is a lot of room for negotiation. As the saying goes, "You don't get what you deserve, you get what you negotiate."

Let's say someone with whom you're in a recreational relationship calls you up and asks you out. Although it would be fun to go out, you have four hours committed to stuffing envelopes, the result of which could further your goal. Rather than automatically saying, "No, I can't make it," present the situation to your friend and see if he or she (let's say he) has any creative solutions.

Maybe he'll offer to come over and help stuff while chatting. This will still take four hours, but it might be more fun. Maybe he will come over and get the work done in two hours, which leaves two newly freed hours for other pursuits. Maybe he will *hire* someone to stuff *all* the envelopes, and you are free for the whole evening. The solutions are endless, and creating them is part of relating.

Saddle your dreams
afore you ride 'em.

MARY WEBB

1881-1927

There are few "pure" relationships—most cross lines, combining one type of relationship with another. Relationships also change over time, evolving—or deteriorating—from one type to another.

It's obvious that—far from being a "loner" as you pursue your goal—you will be relating with many people for many reasons. In fact, you may well be interacting with far more people than you currently are.

Knowing the type of relationships that are available helps you choose the type of relationships that will allow you to best fulfill your dreams.

Father told me that
if I ever met a lady
in a dress like yours,
I must look her
straight in the eyes.

CHARLES, PRINCE OF WALES

(ON SUSAN HAMPSHIRE'S DECOLLETAGÉ)

What Have You Accomplished?

Thus far in this book, we have written thousands and thousands of words. Now it's your turn.

In the next two chapters, we'll ask you to do some writing, as well as some remembering and observing. If you're reading this book for information now and plan to do the "work" later, when you return to do the work, please begin with the chapter *What Is Your Purpose?* and then return to this one.

In doing this exercise, you might want to use 3x5 cards, as that eliminates the need for rewriting. It's not necessary for this exercise, and you'll need a lot of them—200 to 300, probably. If you're low on 3x5 cards (fewer than 300), please save them for the exercises in the chapter *What Do You Want?*

So, what have you accomplished? As things come to mind, set this book aside and write them down (one per card). We'll make some comments to jog your memory, but when it's jogged, write for a while, and then return for some more jogging.

What have you accomplished in your life? What have you achieved? What things did you want and then went out and got? They may be a part of your life now, or they may be long gone. Either way, write them down.

Cars? Jobs? Apartments? Stereos? Furniture? You don't need to list every piece of clothing or can of beans you ever bought, but if some special purchases or exceptional dinners come to mind, write them down.

What about schooling? Did you get a high school diploma? What degrees did you obtain? Perhaps you're prouder of the degrees you *didn't* receive. What about night classes, workshops, seminars or other non-traditional forms of education? Have you learned a language? How to change your own oil (in the car or the kitchen)? Cook? Play ball (any ball)? Dance? Sing? What are your hobbies? Where have you traveled? What about the books

*Dust is a protective coating
for fine furniture.*

MARIO BUATTA

you've read? Plays you've seen? Miniseries you've lived through? Tapes you've listened to?

What about people? Of whom did you say, "I want this person for a friend/lover/boss/employee/teacher/student/roommate/wife/husband/etc.," and got them? Even if you didn't initiate the relationship, for every relationship you've ever had, you had to do *something,* even if it was not saying no.

The fact that a relationship, job—or anything else—may have *ended* poorly doesn't mean it shouldn't be on your list. If it was something you wanted and you got, that counts. Much of our growth comes from getting what we want and finding out we don't want it after all. Even if *they* are the ones who decided it's not what they wanted, include them on your list, too. You had them for a time, and the only difference between a happy ending and an unhappy ending is where they put the closing credits. Go to the happy time, consider it an achievement, and write it down.

What about social or political goals? Did your candidate win? Did the proposal you want pass? Even if you did nothing more than *vote* for it, that's better than half the people in the United States do during any given election. What giving—directly, or through organizations—have you done?

Yes, this is a lot of remembering and a lot of writing. That's the point. People tend to forget what they've accomplished. They tend to forget how much they have created. They tend to forget how powerful they are.

How about family? Did you create any children? What have you done for members of your family? Perhaps *leaving* a family situation that wasn't doing *anyone* any good was a major achievement.

What about health? What illnesses have you successfully recovered from? What changes in your body image have you made? How much weight have you lost? (Some people have lost several thousand pounds. Although it may have gone back on, each pound *was* an accomplishment

One can never consent to creep
when one feels
an impulse to soar.

HELEN KELLER

when it was taken off.) Do you exercise? *Have* you exercised? Take vitamins? Had body work of any kind done? What bad habits have you overcome (even temporarily)? Have you been in therapy? Whatever the outcome, the fact that you sought help is an accomplishment.

What about God? Do you go to church? Temple? Meditate? Pray? Whatever connection you have with the Almighty, *you* had something to do with it. (If not, *everyone* would feel connected, and that's not the case.) Perhaps your accomplishments included abandoning one religious or spiritual path to find one closer to your heart.

Keep writing. The pump has been primed. This is a good time to set this book aside and spend some time writing and remembering. It will never be a complete list—the list of your achievements is nearly endless—but at some point, you'll approach the limit of your immediate memory. Pick up the book again and continue reading when the memories run out.

☆

Now, read through your list. This is a good running list to keep. It's a constant reminder of how much you *have* done, how much you *have* created—and how much more is available to you in the future.

Without regretting anything, imagine what you could have achieved if all these accomplishments had been pointed in a *single* direction—if all this *effective*, creative energy had been directed toward fulfilling your heart's desire.

Again: no regrets. Don't look at the past and say, "What a waste." As Katherine Mansfield suggested, "Make it a rule of life never to regret and never to look back. Regret is an appalling waste of energy; you can't build on it; it's only good for wallowing in."

Rather than regret, use the energy to be *excited* about the future. If you're, say, thirty, don't think, "Thirty

*The world is moving so fast
these days that the man who
says it can't be done
is generally interrupted
by someone doing it.*

HARRY EMERSON FOSDICK

wasted years!" Most people don't begin making their own decisions until eighteen or twenty.

Let's arbitrarily say, "Life begins when you move out of your parents' house." (Although, for you it might be, "Life began when I got my first full-time job," or, if you're, say, Prince Charles and *never* plan to move out of your parents' house, "Life began when I got married.")

At whatever point your adult life began, that's the point to start counting. For the first twenty-or-so years of life, we really are in the hands of other people. If, then, you are thirty, and moved out when you were twenty, you really have ten years of *your* life to consider.

Look at what you've done in those years. Imagine how much you'll accomplish in the next similar period of time. This is something worth getting excited about.

And, shortly, you'll be learning even more techniques on how to focus your goals, how to channel your creative energy toward them, how to move beyond the comfort zone and into the area of living your dreams.

Happiness?
A good cigar, a good meal,
and a good woman
—or a bad woman.
It depends on how much
happiness you can handle.

GEORGE BURNS

What Do You Have?

This list is a subset of the list you just made. It is a list of everything you're glad to have in your life *now*.

This is an exercise in recognizing what we often tend to take for granted. It is also an exercise in *gratitude*.

As you write this Inventory of Now, begin each item on the list with a phrase such as "I am grateful for..." or "I am thankful for..." or simply, "Thank you for..."

The list, then, will read,

> I am grateful for my health
>
> I am grateful for my house
>
> I am grateful for my relationship with _____
>
> and so on.

If you used 3x5 cards for the last exercise, you can go through those and pull out the ones that apply. Write at the top of each "I am grateful for..." or, if the top is already taken, you can add to the bottom, "...for which I am grateful," (or thankful, or any word you prefer).

If you didn't use 3x5 cards, go back over your list and copy those things onto a new list. As you copy to the new list, preface each with "I am grateful for..." or "I am thankful for..."

Please do write "I am grateful for..." before each thing on your list. Writing it once at the top of a page is not as effective—the physical writing of it, over and over, is important. And, if you're doing this process on a computer, for heaven sakes don't program it to add the phrase automatically!

(When we say "things," we mean anything—from people to cars to body parts to inner qualities to God. We don't mean to diminish any of them by calling them "things." We found "things" is the best word to encompass individual units of anything.)

After transferring all the things from the list of your accomplishments, take a look at your current life. What

If I had known my son
was going to be
president of Bolivia,
I would have taught him to
read and write.

ENRIQUE PENARANDA'S MOTHER

did you leave out? What was so taken for granted you didn't include it on your list of achievements? What would you miss if it were taken from you? List those things, too.

What about your body are you grateful for? Even if some part of it doesn't look the way you'd like or function the way you want, what about the rest of it? Be grateful for those parts, and add them to your list.

How about your abilities? What do you know how to do that you're glad to know? Don't forget the skills you currently use to make money, the skills you *plan* to make money with, and the qualities that keep your friends coming back for more. (You can review the list of qualities you made while working on your purpose.)

Speaking of friends, what about people? Who are the friends, lovers, acquaintances, spouses, children, relatives, coworkers, fellow-seekers, etc. you're glad to have in your life?

What about physical possessions? What do you own (or have access to) you like? Look around. Your insurance agent may have recommended you make a list of this sort for years. Now's a good time to do it.

What about hobbies? Sports? The view from your window? The country, state, city, and neighborhood you live in? What freedoms do you have you'd hate to lose?

And what about God? In addition to all the direct thanks one can give The Diety, what about the organizations, books and people who relay the spiritual and religious teaching you appreciate?

This is another of those lists that takes some time. It is, however, finite, and, with some time spent on it, can become fairly complete.

It is time well spent.

*The truth is that all of us
attain the greatest success
and happiness possible in this
life whenever we use our
native capacities to
their greatest extent.*

DR. SMILEY BLANTON

Choice and Consequences

We've already seen how life is like *The Wheel of Fortune* and *Jeopardy*. Well, life is also like *Truth or Consequences*. When we tell ourselves the *truth* about our life, we are better prepared to take the *consequences*.

One of the areas in which people often fail to tell themselves the truth is the area of choices. Many people *pretend* they have made Choice A, while their actions, behavior and direction clearly indicate they are moving toward Choice B. When they arrive at B (or see it looming before them), they react with genuine surprise (often coupled with disappointment and/or outrage), "What's this B stuff? I chose A!"

It's one thing to tell *others* we're heading toward A when *we* know we're heading toward B. That's called *tactics*. It's quite another to tell *ourselves* we're heading toward A, when all the while we're making a beeline for B. That's called *confusion, frustration* and *what's-a-nice-person-like-me-doing-in-a-life-like-this?*

The thing that gets us to our goal is *action*—action in the broadest sense of the word. Mental action, emotional action and physical action—all focused in one direction —gets us to our goal. People tell themselves they want one thing—then they think, feel and move toward another.

Why?

The fear of The Consequences.

Humans are smart—as compared with, say, amoebas. Humans can logically, and fairly accurately, project ahead in time. If we go to the store, we know we will find popsicles there. If we pay a certain amount of money, we can have a popsicle of our own. If we put it in our mouth, it will taste cold and sweet. If we set forth on that course, in all probability, that is precisely what will happen.

We can also predict the down side of the future—the potentially negative consequences of the action: it will cost

*Far better it is
to dare mighty things,
to win glorious triumphs even
though checkered by failure,
than to rank with those poor
spirits who neither enjoy
nor suffer much
because they live in the gray
twilight that knows neither
victory nor defeat.*

THEODORE ROOSEVELT

money, it will take time, it will contain so many extra calories, it might spoil our appetite, and so on.

When we consider actually moving toward our heart's desire, a part of us automatically looks ahead to the possible consequences—especially the negative ones. The comfort zone gloms onto these negative consequences. The comfort zone argues it's the *actions* that will bring on the negative *consequences*. The comfort zone's emotionally backed recommendation: No Action.

The comfort zone stays fairly quiet as long as we don't seriously contemplate action. We can *want* our dream all we want; we can *think about someday getting it* as much as we like; we can *tell everyone we know how we're one day going to have it* at every opportunity. We can even *make commitments we don't really plan to keep*. The only thing we can't do is DO IT!

If we begin to do it, the comfort zone goes into overdrive—hyperdrive, actually—and gets us back on track. "On track" to the comfort zone is what we've always done before, which means heading (again) toward B, even though our dream rests with A.

Why are the consequences of action so uncomfortable? Let's take a look:

1. *When we choose, we must let other choices go.* If we have enough money for one popsicle, and we choose cherry, we must let go of grape, orange, tangerine, banana supreme, pina colada, watermelon, tutti-fruti and passion fruit. Naturally, we don't *want* to let go of grape, orange, tangerine, banana supreme, pina colada, watermelon, tutti-fruti and passion fruit. All that loss! We're miserable. We should have stayed at home. No, the storekeeper won't let us have a bite of each. No, there's no credit. We keep picking up and setting down one flavor after another, feeling rotten, until we get frostbite.

   When we make our Big Choice and go for the Big Dream, it means letting go of all the other Big Dreams, even though those dreams may be as

*Procrastination is the
fear of success.
People procrastinate because
they are afraid of the success
that they know will result if
they move ahead now.
Because success is heavy,
carries a responsibility with it,
it is much easier to
procrastinate and live on the
"someday I'll" philosophy.*

DENIS WAITLEY

appealing as grape, orange, tangerine, banana supreme, pina colada, watermelon, tutti-fruti and passion fruit. We don't like hearing this news any more than you do, but if we don't tell it to you, life will. (Life probably already has.)

If we make *no choice,* we end up with *nothing.* (Actually, we end up with what randomly comes our way that's "not too bad." Compared with *any* of our Big Dreams, however, it's nothing. *And* we have to pay for it, just as though it were a Big One.)

2. *When we choose, we risk losing.* If we boldly walk into the store and say, "I want a cherry popsicle," we run the risk of the storekeeper saying, "We're all out," or, even worse, "We sold the last one five minutes ago. You *just missed it."* (Why do people *say* things like that? Why do they add torture to torment? We don't know why, but they do.)

If we commit to the Big One, the Big Dream, we might not get it. We might lose. And not only will *we* know, but *everyone else* will know, too. It's the "agony of defeat." Ugh! How horrible. When we never really choose—never really commit—if we don't get it, we can always say, "Oh, I didn't really want it anyway."

3. *When we choose, we risk winning.* We stride in! We put down our money! We get the cherry popsicle! We claim it! It is in our hand! It is ours! The storekeeper says, "Congratulations!" Now what?

It's the Big Now-What? that many people find more intimidating than "the agony of defeat." Defeat is part of most people's comfort zone. But *winning?* "What would I do? What would happen to me? How would I cope?" It's called the fear of success.

Not only do we have to make changes to become successful, but success itself brings additional changes. The greater the success, the greater the changes. Imagine being very, *very* successful at something. Would you live where you're living now?

Quit now, you'll never make it.
If you disregard this advice,
you'll be halfway there.

DAVID ZUCKER

Would you do the same things, go the same places, wear the same clothes, have all the same friends? Would *any* part of your life be the same?

Even more startling than the outer changes, however, are the inner changes brought on by success. What do we do with the concept we have that we're not *worthy* of success? How about the cultural programming most of us have that we're just an "ordinary person"? How can an ordinary person be capable of *extra*ordinary success? What's wrong with this picture?

An even deeper reason we fear success is that we fear our own power. We are much more powerful than we let ourselves believe. If we knew how powerful we were, "the slings and arrows of outrageous fortune" would be about as troublesome as being attacked by a frustrated two-year-old.

This sense of personal power is not comfortable. It's much easier to believe the cultural conditioning that things "out there" affect us "in here;" that what happens to us is inseparably linked with how we feel; that dreams don't come true; and that our lot in life is not to have a lot in life—so get used to it.

☆

So, what do we do about all this? Some suggestions:

1. Know it's there. Know what happens when you make choices, and be prepared for the consequences. *Expect* the comfort zone to act up. That's its job.

2. Be prepared to let go of grape, orange, tangerine, banana supreme, pina colada, watermelon, tutti-fruti and passion fruit *for now*. Make your slogan, "Cherry today, tutti-fruti tomorrow!" Success in one

Always listen to experts.
They'll tell you what
can't be done and why.
Then do it.

ROBERT HEINLEIN

area quite often clears pathways for success—both inner and outer—in several others. If cherry is the one you want most *now,* get that. Later look around and choose again.

3. If we choose, we *may* lose, but if we don't choose, we almost *certainly* lose. This is if we define losing as not getting what we want. Some people tell themselves, "If I don't play, I can't lose." As long as I don't lose, they say, "then everything's OK." The problem with the system of not losing is that you can *never win.* Realize that the risk of losing is part of winning, but *never* losing means never getting what we want.

4. Accept the fact that winning is not all it's cracked up to be—*but what else is there?* Would you rather be in the store, eating your popsicle, saying, "This doesn't taste quite cherry enough to me," or be outside the store, your nose pressed against the window, thinking how wonderful it must be to be able to afford a popsicle?

5. Know that you are worthy. (We're all worthy of our dream.) Yes, you *are* special. (We all have a special dream, the doing of which will make us special to a great many people.)

6. You are powerful. Sorry. Hate to be the bearer of bad news. You are. You can continue arm wrestling with yourself, or you can use both arms, your whole heart, and all your strength to wrestle with greatness.

The choice is yours.

What's money?
A man is a success if he
gets up in the morning
and goes to bed at night
and in between does what he
wants to do.

BOB DYLAN

The Myth of Money, Fame and Power

Money, fame, and power—for their own sake—all spell one thing: *glamour.*

Glamour is one of the biggest traps in life. It is a sweet, sticky snare, like the petals of a Venus-flytrap. "Come to me," it beckons, "All happiness lies here."

What lies there are lies. It all rests on the myth we discussed earlier—that someone or something outside us can make us happy; that we are somehow incomplete without certain externals; and that if we have enough certain externals, we will never be unhappy again.

"You don't seem to realize that a poor person who is unhappy is in a better position than a rich person who is unhappy," explained Jean Kerr. "Because the poor person has hope. He thinks money would help."

Money, fame and power, as intentions, are deadly. People pursue them, get them, are not happy (in fact, are usually more unhappy). Then they decide, "It must not be *enough.* I need more, *then* I'll be happy." So they set their sights higher, get more of the thing that didn't make them happy in the first place, and are unhappier still.

As with any addictive substance, by now they're hooked. Life becomes the relentless pursuit of more! More! *More!*

Are we saying money, fame and power are intrinsically evil? No. They have their place. They are tools—*methods* for obtaining other goals. As goals themselves, however, they are nothing. Less than nothing. Distractions at best; addictions at worst.

Take money, for example. Let's say we're hungry and we don't have any money. We think, "If I only had money, I could eat. I want some money. I'm hungry and I want some money." So, someone says he'll give us all the money we could want, and locks us in a room with one million dollars in cash. Now what? Are we still hungry? Yes. Do we have lots of money? Yes. Perhaps a few lower forms of life that thrive on paper and ink could find

Pleasure is a shadow,
wealth is vanity,
and power a pageant;
but knowledge
is ecstatic in enjoyment,
perennial in frame,
unlimited in space and
indefinite in duration.

DE WITT CLINTON

nourishment there, but within a few weeks we would probably trade the whole pile for a hamburger.

That's what it's like to go after money for money's sake. You get the money, and then what? "I'd see the world." Then make seeing the world your goal. If money is the necessary method for doing that, fine. It will come. There could, however, be lots of other methods. You could, for example, meet someone who wants to hire a traveling companion and *get paid* to see the world.

"I've had an exciting life," Rose Kennedy wrote. "I married for love and got a little money along with it." That's another method. Of course, *do* marry for love. Remember the old saying, "The one who marries for money, earns it."

"Money won't buy happiness," Bill Vaughan said, "but it will pay the salaries of a huge research staff to study the problem."

Some people who want to, say, write a book, wonder how to get the money so they can buy a word processor. When we point out to them that several very fine books were written before the advent of computers, they usually frown and say, "You don't understand."

We *do* understand. We were writing books back when the *cheapest* computer cost a million dollars. Did we wait to get a million dollars before writing? No. We wrote with the "word processor" at hand—a pen. Shakespeare didn't even have that. He used a *quill*.

Many people use money as the *rational lie* for not doing something they want to do. It sounds *so good*. "As soon as I get the money to _____, I'll be living my dream!" Other people listening to these excuses believe them, because they, too, have their collection of rational lies. It's a conspiracy: I won't challenge your rational lies if you don't challenge mine.

"When you do what you love, the money follows," is probably a phrase you've heard before. It's true, but incomplete.

*I don't know much about
being a millionaire,
but I'll bet I'd be <u>darling</u> at it.*

DOROTHY PARKER

The complete statement is, "When you do what you love, the *necessary* money will follow." The money that's *needed* to fulfill your goal will appear, in the proper timing, as you prove yourself worthy (that is, as you do the work necessary to fulfill that goal). What will *not* appear is all the money that would be nice and make everything all comfortable and cozy to do what you love in precisely the moment you want it.

If you want to write a book, you will, for a start, have enough money to buy a pencil, a notebook, and be given fifteen free minutes each day. If you use the fifteen minutes each day writing, when you fill the notebook, you will have enough money for another notebook and be given thirty minutes a day. And so on. Eventually, you'll have a book. What will the person have who's waiting for a computer before even beginning to write? Waiting.

To make the phrase "Do what you love and the necessary money will follow," even *more* accurate, we'd say, "Do what you love, and the necessary *resources* will follow."

In some cases, it will be money. In other cases, it will be time. It might be information, tools, connections, opportunities—the list is endless. Another word for *resources*, of course, is *methods*.

It's the same with fame. If fame is the natural result of doing what you love to do, then so be it. Most famous people consider fame a burden. The "burden of fame" is something of a joke, of course. "A celebrity is a person who works hard all his life to become well known," said Fred Allen, "then wears dark glasses to avoid being recognized."

Funny side aside, however, imagine not being able to go *anywhere* without being *mobbed*. It may sound nice, and for a time it might be fun, but, after a while, you'd probably agree with Lewis Grizzard: "Being a newspaper columnist is like being married to a nymphomaniac. It's great for the first two weeks."

"If I were famous," some not-famous people say, "I'd get on TV and raise money to feed the homeless." A double-glamour whammy! *Fame* to get *money* to get something

*Fame is only good
for one thing—
they will cash your check
in a small town.*

TRUMAN CAPOTE

done. To anyone saying this, we suggest: If feeding the homeless is your calling, go out and feed *one* homeless person *now*. Tomorrow, feed two. Keep it up. Maybe you'll become famous for that. If so, use it as a tool. If not, at least you'll be fulfilling your dream. As Mother Teresa said, "We can do no great things—only small things with great love."

You can easily see how power enters into the glamour trap. What's the point of power if you don't use it for something? Nothing. So, what is the something you would do if you had the power? Then go do that. "Do the thing and you will have the Power," Emerson explained.

No, it may not be as grand, sweeping and dramatic as our imagination might conjure, but if you don't get satisfaction from doing it on a small scale, you won't get any more satisfaction doing it on a global scale. Nothing, multiplied by five billion, is still nothing.

*Men for the sake of
getting a living
forget to live.*

MARGARET FULLER

(1810-1850)

The Myth of the 40-Hour Work Week

Most people think they "need" to work forty hours per week. For some, that's true. For others, it's sixty hours per week. For still others, eighty. (Ask any spouse whose "job" it is to care for the house, or creative person working on a project, or monk in a monastery, or social activist working for change). For some others, it might be five or ten.

Just as "the work expands to fill the time available," so, too, the "needs" expand to consume the money available. ("Expenditure rises to meet income."—C. Northcote Parkinson.) If we are bringing home forty-hours' worth of money, we will spend it. As John Guare pointed out, "The rich live hand-to-mouth, too—just on a higher level." If that forty-hours' worth of work amounts to $150 or $1,500 or $15,000 or $150,000, or $1,500,000—it will be spent.

Many people are trapped in the myth of a 40-hour work week.

If we define "job" as what we do that we don't really want to do to get money to do what we really want to do (reread it a few times—it makes sense), then the number of *hours* we work depends upon (A) what it cost us to do what we want to do, and (B) how much per hour we get.

What about our basic needs? Good question! Basic needs are often dictated by what we want to do. For example, someone who wants to pray all day and serve God might be able to combine that with life in a monastery and not have to work for even *one* hour per week at the local fast-food emporium.

Someone wanting to make global changes could find the same all-expenses-paid fulfillment of a goal in the Peace Corps, or, if they wanted to do it domestically, in VISTA. The examples go on and on.

The meeting of our basic needs should be based on the fulfillment of our heart's desire, not on the latest style, or how to intensely fill the few "leisure" hours we have when not working at a job we hate.

*Never keep up
with the Joneses.
Drag them down to your level.
It's cheaper.*

QUENTIN CRISP

To significantly raise your standard of living sometimes requires significantly lowering it for a while. Say you want to write a book, and you have a $25,000 car and a $2,000 per month apartment. You don't need those to write a book. A $5,000 car (or even a $500 moped) and a $500 per month apartment is all you need.

"Yes, but..."

Do we hear the comfort zone on the rise?

People who plan to "make it" had better plan to sacrifice—and that *starts* with creature comforts. It might mean a smaller living space, bringing in a roommate, or turning the current living space into an office. Either way—discomfort, ho! It may mean fewer dinners out with friends, fewer trips, fewer new clothes, not as many CD's, domestic wines, domestic sparkling water (aka club soda), domestic pasta, domestic vinegar—and no domestics.

Remember the New England maxim? "Use it up, wear it out, make it do, or do without." Do without what? Oh, just our dreams.

One of the toughest things to sacrifice is the idea that we *should* be comfortable all the time. We only said you would find *satisfaction* pursuing your dreams, not comfort.

When we want all the creature comforts the Joneses have, we trade our *time* for those comforts—the time we spend at a job making money that may be keeping us from living our dreams. Time is precious. It is given each day in equal measure to us all. What we do with that time determines what we achieve in our lives.

TIME = DREAMS

Also, let go of the myth that we only have one career, profession, marriage, religious belief, etc. per lifetime. Person after person has demonstrated (in some areas you may be one of them) that this is simply not true. Or that there is a certain *age* at which you can begin any of these.

This is your *life*—not a myth. Let your life be one that *inspires* myth making—don't make your life a slave to the myths of the past.

*In the afternoons, Gertrude Stein and
I used to go antique hunting in the
local shops, and I remember once
asking her if she thought
I should become a writer.
In the typically cryptic way we were
all enchanted with, she said, "No."
I took that to mean yes and sailed for
Italy the next day.*

WOODY ALLEN

You have to know what you want to get.

GERTRUDE STEIN

What Do You Want?

Here it is, the chapter you've been looking forward to—with eagerness, anxiety or both. Here, you'll discover what *you* want. You'll get to choose which of those wants you'll pursue, which you'll let pass, and which you'll postpone.

The underlying question of this chapter was best stated by Dr. Robert Schuller, "What would you attempt to do if you knew you could not fail?"

The answer to this question may require some reflection. We use the word "reflection" rather than "thought" because, as William James once said, "A great many people think they are thinking when they are merely re-arranging their prejudices."

We all have prejudices. We think we don't know what we want, and that becomes a prejudice. We think we know *for sure* what we want, and that becomes a prejudice. We think we'll discover what we want sometime—but not now—and that becomes a prejudice.

To the degree you can, clear the slate. Start fresh. If a dream is truly your dream, it will survive the questions we are about to put to you. If it is not your time to know, nothing we can ask will part the veil. You and your dream are safe. How well you learn about your dream in this process is entirely up to you.

If you happen to have some 3x5 cards lying around (ha!), get them. And a pen or pencil. If you're not using 3x5 cards, get three pads or piles of paper and make lists. Without 3x5 cards, you'll have to do a bit more recopying.

Let's start by returning to the sanctuary.

Imagine going to the entryway. It opens for you. You step inside and bathe under the pure, white light just inside the entryway. You know that only that which is for your highest good can take place while you are in your sanctuary, and during this process.

It's important to ask this for, as Cicero said, "the highest good." It's usual for various glamour-seeking parts of

*The only way
to avoid being miserable
is not to have enough leisure
to wonder whether you are
happy or not.*

GEORGE BERNARD SHAW

us to want something, not because *we* want it, but because it would be impressive to have. Obtaining these things only leads to woe. As St. Theresa of Avila said, "More tears are shed over answered prayers than unanswered ones." Or, to quote Oscar Wilde, "When the gods choose to punish us, they merely answer our prayers."

Asking for the highest good of all concerned allows your true dreams to surface. In that way, when our prayers are answered, they need only invoke tears of joy.

Go to the People Mover and invite in your Master Teacher. See your Master Teacher appear through the white light of the People Mover. Welcome your Master Teacher. Chat for a while about the process you are about to do.

This is a special process using your sanctuary. You can open your eyes, write things down, do things, and when you close your eyes again, you're immediately back in the sanctuary, precisely where you were when you opened your eyes. In fact, this entire process is done *in* the sanctuary—some of it with your eyes open, some with your eyes closed.

Open your eyes. You're about to make three piles of cards (or three lists). Each card will contain one item. As you write each item, place it in the appropriate pile.

Write a card to identify each pile. The first is labeled "WANTS," the second "QUALITIES and ABILITIES," and the third "LIMITATIONS."

Now, start filling out the cards. Free associate. A WANT ("Move to New York") might spark some of your QUALITIES and ABILITIES ("Adventurous," "Flexible," "Cultured"), and also some LIMITATIONS ("Not enough money," "Fear," "Leaving friends behind").

An ABILITY ("Talented") might prompt a WANT ("Become an opera singer"), which may inspire a LIMITATION ("Too much work").

Once a card has been filled out on a given subject, it need not be repeated. One "fear" card, for example, is

We must select the illusion
which appeals
to our temperament and
embrace it with passion,
if we want to be happy.

CYRIL CONNOLLY

enough. (Might as well fill that one out right now and get it over with.)

Don't bother sorting or prioritizing the cards. If you "want" a hot fudge sundae, write it down. And, despite the rattlings of an earlier chapter, if money, fame and power pop into your mind, by all means fill a card with them (three cards, in fact).

Tiny Tim, in listing his wants, said, "I'd love to see Christ come back to crush the spirit of hate and make men put down their guns. I'd also like just one more hit single." That's how our wants seem to go—some cosmic and grand; others personal and, well, tiny.

In the process of decision-making and organization, putting it *all* down in writing is known as a "data dump." Dump all the data onto cards, and the only sorting to be concerned about now is whether something is a WANT, a QUALITY and ABILITY, or a LIMITATION.

In writing all this down, remember that you're not committing to any of it. You'll have the opportunity to do that in a later chapter. For the purposes of this chapter, everything is just a "good idea."

And don't forget to have fun. Yes, it's your life you're looking at, and what you'll be doing with it, but that doesn't mean you have to be too *serious*. What we do to fill the time between our first cry and our last sigh is all a game, anyway. Treat this list with the same gravity you'd spend deciding what to do next Saturday afternoon. Shall we play football, baseball or stage a ballet?

Spend some time now and fill out the cards. If you "run out," close your eyes and return to the sanctuary. Ask the Master Teacher for suggestions. Take your time with this process. Get all your WANTS, QUALITIES and ABILITIES, and LIMITATIONS on cards. Spend at least an hour doing this, although you may choose to take longer.

Do it till it's done, and return to this place in the book when your piles (or lists) are complete.

You've got to be very careful
if you don't know
where you are going,
because you might not
get there.

YOGI BERRA

Excellent. Congratulations.

Now go through the cards (or list) you made during the earlier process *What Is Your Purpose?* Write your purpose on a card and place it where you can easily see it. Does this remind you of other WANTS, QUALITIES and ABILITIES or LIMITATIONS? When you discovered your purpose, you made a list of qualities about yourself, and also actions you enjoyed. These can be added to the QUALITIES and ABILITIES or WANTS piles.

Now, look at the earlier listing of all the things you already have for which you are grateful. Those things you want to include in your future, add them to your WANTS list. Yes, you already have them, but *maintaining* them will probably take some time.

Almost *everything*—except perhaps that rock you brought back from Yosemite—requires *some* maintenance. To *maintain* what you currently have must be considered a goal for the future. So, add "Maintain house," "Maintain car," "Maintain relationship with _____," etc. to your pile of WANTS. If any ABILITIES and QUALITIES or LIMITATIONS arise while adding these wants, make cards for them, too.

Let's turn to the WANT pile. Sort each want into one of five categories: Marriage/Family, Career/Professional, Social/Political, Religious/Spiritual, and Recreation/Fun.

We are making the assumption that *everyone* will want *some* recreation and/or fun in their lives regardless of which area of life they choose to primarily pursue. It seems to us that even the most serious devotee of a given path will want *some* recreation—in the sense of re-creation. So we're making this a *parallel* category, one that can complement whatever major life area you choose to pursue.

In choosing the category (Marriage/Family, Career/Professional, Social/Political, Religious/Spiritual, Recreation/Fun) in which to put each WANT, remember, "to thine own self be true." There may be an *obvious*

There is no security
on this earth,
there is only opportunity.

GENERAL DOUGLAS MACARTHUR

category, but your personal *motivation* may make it part of another category.

If one of your WANTS is, say, "Become a minister," is that because you want to be closer to God (Religious/Spiritual), you feel it would be a good platform from which to make social change (Social/Political), you think it would be a rewarding occupation (Career/Professional), or you want to intensify your relationship with someone who has a decided fondness for persons of the cloth (Marriage/Family)?

We must look closely at our motivations. As Madonna explained, "Losing my virginity was a career move."

You could, for example, put "Get married" under Career/Professional because everyone in the career you intend to pursue is properly espoused. Or, perhaps you're doing it for Religious/Spiritual reasons, following the dictate of Paul when he wrote, "It is better to marry than to burn." (I Corinthians, 7:9) You could be getting married for primarily societal reasons: "Any young man who is unmarried at the age of twenty-one," said Brigham Young, "is a menace to the community." Or, you might want to get married just because you want to get married (Marriage/Family).

There will be overlapping, of course, but put each WANT card in the category that *most* fits your motivation.

That done, review each of the Marriage/Family, Career/Professional, Social/Political, and Religious/Spiritual categories. (We'll look at Recreation/Fun a little later.)

Now, let's look ahead for the next, say, five years.

Take each category of wants separately, read them over, and then close your eyes. Imagine what your life would be like in the next five years if you had a goodly number of those wants. Explore both the good *and* the bad, the up side and the down. Be neither too romantic nor too cynical. Take a look at it "straight on."

Use all the elements of your sanctuary to explore your life in that category. You can use the **People Mover** to

*JANE HATHAWAY: Chief,
haven't you ever heard of the
saying "It's not whether you
win or lose,
it's how you play the game"?
MR. DRYSDALE: Yes, I've
heard it.
And I consider it
one of the most ridiculous
statements ever made.*

THE BEVERLY HILLBILLIES

invite experts in the field and discuss the pros and cons; the **Information Retrieval System** to gather any facts or data you might find useful; the **Video Screen** to see yourself living that life; put on **Ability Suits** for each of the wants, and experience what that ability is like in the **Ability Suit Practice Area;** visit your **Health Center** and check on the health risks and advantages of each want; contemplate the category in your **Sacred Room;** and, of course, take your **Master Teacher** along with you throughout the whole process, discussing your reactions as you go.

And in all cases, ask yourself, "Would this life fulfill my purpose?"

After spending time in your sanctuary with each of the four main areas of life, ask yourself, "During the next five years, within which *category* does my heart's desire lie? During the next five years, which would give me the most satisfaction?"

If no answer is forthcoming, return with your Master Teacher to your sanctuary and explore. Is the choice between two? Examine them both, alternately. Which is most "on purpose"? Which category thrills your heart the most?

When you've chosen the category, go through all the wants within the category and select the one WANT you want the most. Again, use all the tools in the sanctuary to explore the pros and cons of each WANT, and choose the Big Want, the one thing you want most.

Why do we have you choose a category first, then a goal within that category? Usually, going for the Big Goal within a category automatically fulfills many of the smaller goals within that category—not all, of course, but many. If you pick the *area* of life first, you will, by pursuing a Big Dream within that area, have more of what you want in the area of life you choose.

You are, of course, free to choose a Big Dream *outside* the area of life you are most drawn to. We have found, however, that most people tend to be happier and more

*I always wanted to
be somebody,
but I should have been
more specific.*

LILY TOMLIN

fulfilled by obtaining several goals within the area they prefer, rather than one big goal in an area they don't prefer as much. This is just an observation. Please make your choice of Big Dream yourself. Your Master Teacher will not steer you wrong.

One method of choosing between two Big Dreams that *seem* equally appealing is to make a list of all the pros and cons for each choice. In reading over these lists and comparing them, one usually takes the lead.

Is this it? Is this your dream? The Big Dream? If yes, read on. If no, continue choosing.

When you have chosen, then *quantify* your dream. That is, make it a goal with *specific results* so that you'll know when you've achieved it.

This can be tough. People like to keep their dreams vague. "I want a family," is easier to say than, "I want a spouse, two children and a rottweiler." As you can see, however, one is obtainable, one is not.

"I want a family" is not obtainable because the goal does not define what a family is. You could have a family of mice in your kitchen and your goal is fulfilled. "That's not what I mean." You could have 18 children and *still* not reach the goal, because some families have 19 children. "That's not what I mean, either."

What *do* you mean?

Put something countable, something quantifiable in your goal so that you'll *know* when you've obtained it. You are not stuck with this goal forever and ever. When you reach it, you can make it bigger. For now, however, it's important to know what your goal is, and be able to tell when you've reached it. And remember: you haven't committed to anything yet.

Here is where money often comes in. Although money is not a great goal *by itself,* as an indicator of whether or not you've obtained a goal, it can be excellent. As the people who understand money say, "Money is just a way of keeping score."

*Ours is a world where people
don't know what they want
and are willing to go
through hell to get it.*

DON MARQUIS

Rather than, "I want to be a singer," say "I want to be a singer making $50,000 (or $100,000, or $1,000,000) per year singing." Make the goal big enough to be a dream (if you're already making $40,000 at something, $42,000 is hardly a Big Dream), but small enough to be at least *partially* believable (if you're making nothing at something, jumping to $100,000,000 per year might be a bit too much for any part of you to believe).

Some goals are quantifiable by time. "I want to spend six months per year traveling." Others by amount. "I want to weigh 150 pounds." Others by degrees or recognition. "I want my Chiropractic certification."

In setting a goal, it's fun to remember the movie *Bedazzled*. In a reworking of Faust, Peter Cook plays the devil, and Dudley Moore—a short-order cook—sells his soul to be with the waitress who is indifferent to him. The devil catches the cook in one loophole after another. Moore wants to be married to his beloved, live in the country and be rich. He gets his wish. *However,* she is in love with someone else. He asks for another chance. This time he wants to live in the country and have his beloved in love with him, too. The devil finds a loophole and makes them both nuns in a convent. And on it goes.

Be careful of the loopholes. If in doubt, add, "...for the highest good," to the end of your goal.

Write down your goal, your Big Dream.

Now, for a slight aside. Do you know how many minutes there are in a week? 10,080. That's 168 hours. That's your wealth in time. What you spend it on is your choice. No matter what you spend it on, however, you never get more than 10,080 minutes (168 hours) per week.

On a clean sheet of paper, or a new set of cards, write "168 Hours" at the top. Now, let's plan the next year.

Let's start with the basics. How many hours do you sleep each night? Multiply that times seven, and subtract that total from the week. If you sleep eight hours per night, eight hours times seven days is 56 hours per week of sleep.

Time is the thing
that keeps everything from
happening all at once
at the same time.

Subtract that from 168, and you have 112 hours remaining in the week.

Now, how many hours do you spend bathing, shaving, making up, dressing and other ablutions? One hour? Multiply that times seven and subtract from 112. That gives us 105 hours.

And now, eating. An hour a day? More? Less? Consider an average week and see how much time you spend preparing, consuming and cleaning up after eating. Let's say it's an hour per day, or seven hours per week. That's seven from 105, which leaves us with 98 hours.

What about other necessary personal tasks? (Include things *only* if you *actually do them* on a *consistent* basis.) Cleaning (including car and laundry)? Shopping (including groceries)? Working out? Medical appointments or activities? Church? Meditation? And so on. Calculate how much time you spend per week on these (don't forget transportation to and from each), and subtract that from your total.

Let's say all that came to 18 hours per week. That leaves you with 80 hours per week. *Half* the week spent maintaining the *basics*—and thus far we haven't even considered *work!*

We are, by the way, smack dab in the middle of something most people have a *very* difficult time facing: time. Yes, it's easy to accept the *concept* that there's "only so much time to go around," but, when faced with the reality —and the *limitation*—of time *in one's own life,* that's tough.

It is, however, precisely what we're asking you to do. We know that the comfort zone puts on a full-scale extravaganza about this point, but, please, stick with it. It may be uncomfortable, but not as uncomfortable as looking back on this coming year, after it has past, and saying, "I really *meant* to do that, but, where did the time go?"

Now, go through the cards that list the things you already have and would like to maintain. Calculate how much time it would take each week to maintain each of them. Write that figure on the card. Do it for what you

Rule A: Don't.
Rule A1: Rule A does not exist.
Rule A2: Do not discuss the
existence or non-existence of
Rules A, A1 or A2.

R. D. LAING

already have in *all* categories, but keep the cards within each category (the *Marriage/Family* cards in the *Marriage/Family* pile, etc.).

Some things may have zero maintenance (that rock from Yosemite). Others may have quite a lot (children, spouse, careers, major projects). Remember, these are the things you already *have*.

Don't forget to include those things that must be *paid for* to be maintained—mortgage or rental, car payments, etc. For those, calculate the number of hours you must work per week, at your current level of income, to pay for them. For example, if you make $10 per hour, and your car payment, gas and maintenance is $320 per month, that's $80 per week, or eight hours per week to keep the car.

Now the truly tough choices begin.

After all these hours are calculated, go through the cards of what you have and want to maintain, and compare each with the Big Dream you selected. For each item, ask yourself, "Which is more important?"

If what you want to maintain is more important, put that in one pile. Subtract the number of hours it takes to maintain this from the remaining hours in the week. If the Big Dream is more important, put the card of what you want to maintain back in the category pile it originally came from. For the Recreation/Fun category, you can set aside so many hours per week for various activities within the entire category. Subtract that from the hours remaining in the week.

Confused? Don't be surprised. These are difficult choices, and confusion, anger, fear, guilt, unworthiness, hurt feelings, discouragement and all the other denizens of the comfort zone form a marching band when difficult choices present themselves. "You don't have to make these," they counsel, "They will make themselves," or "You need more information," or "Let's take a drive and come back later."

A musician must make music,
an artist must paint,
a poet must write,
if he is to be ultimately
at peace with himself.

ABRAHAM MASLOW

We suggest, however, that you press on. Close your eyes. Get solace and encouragement from your Master Teacher.

Now calculate the cost for *basic necessities* (food, shelter, video rentals) not covered by the things that you already have that you want to keep. How many hours each week will it take to make that much money? Subtract that from your total.

How many hours do you have left? Is this enough to fulfill your Big Dream? If you don't have *at least* fourteen hours per week—two hours per day—to spend on your Big Dream, that may not be enough. If your dream can really come true with *less* investment of time, it might be a rather small Big Dream.

Of course, you can set aside *more* than fourteen hours for your Big Dream. The more time you spend, the more quickly your Dream will come true.

Now comes the fun part. Take your Big Dream, and see how many WANTS would *automatically* (or almost automatically) be fulfilled by achieving the Big Dream. For example, if your Big Dream was to become a movie star, the smaller wants of "Live in Los Angeles," "Be famous," "Make $1,000,000," and "Meet Brooke Shields," would naturally follow. That is, in fulfilling the Big Dream, the smaller dreams would almost effortlessly come to pass.

It's OK to go into *any* of the piles and pull out dreams that fit within the Big Dream. Be honest, now. With enough bending and twisting, almost *anything* can fit behind a big enough dream. "I want to be an airline pilot, so watching every movie that comes out will better help me tell the passengers what the movie is about on board the plane," or "I want to write a novel about being rich, so I think I'll take all my money and buy a Rolls Royce so I can get in the mood." Things like that.

Now, back to the tough part. *Eliminate* all wants that are in *direct opposition* to your Big Dream. "Live in New York City" and "Experience the joys of small town life" do not belong in the same dream. One of them must go.

*The method of the enterprising
is to plan with audacity,
and execute with vigor;
to sketch out
a map of possibilities;
and then to treat them
as probabilities.*

BOVEE

Be ruthless on this one. "Oh, I can stay in Kansas and become a movie star." Uh-huh.

Please remember that simultaneously pursuing Big Dreams from two different categories is difficult. If, for example, your main area of activity is *not* Marriage/Family, please keep this in mind: if the romantic relationship you may seek *in addition to* your Big Dream does not provide you with *more time* to pursue your dream, either your Big Dream, or the relationship, will suffer. Usually both. We don't like this harsh reality any more than you do. It seems, however, to be the way it is.

If you still have time in your week (which is doubtful), you can add other wants to your week *providing* they are not in opposition to your Big Dream. The smart thing is to choose additional goals that somehow support or enhance the Big Dream—but as soon as you run out of hours, stop. That's it.

You can now combine the piles of The Big Dream And All That Comes With It and the pile of things already in your life you chose to maintain. Review your choices. Behold: your next year (and probably beyond).

Write at the top of each card in the new pile the following: "I am going to..." No longer are these things mere wants. They are directions, intentions, inevitabilities.

Of those remaining WANTS not in the *I am going to...* pile—hold onto them. We'll get to them in the next chapter.

For now, review the LIMITATIONS pile. For each limitation, ask yourself how you can turn it into an *advantage*. How can it become an *ally* in fulfilling your Big Dream? We've already looked at fear becoming the energy to do your best in a new situation, guilt as the energy for personal change, unworthiness as a way of keeping on track, hurt feelings as a way of remembering the caring, anger as the energy for change, and discouragement as a reminder of our courage.

See if you can find a *positive use* for everything on your list. Impatience? Be impatient for success. Stubborn? Let it become determination. Big ego? Put it behind your

There's nothing to winning, really.
That is, if you happen to be blessed
with a keen eye, and agile mind,
and no scruples whatsoever.

ALFRED HITCHCOCK

One should always play fairly
when one has the winning cards.

OSCAR WILDE

goal. Laziness? Become lazy about doing the things *not* on the way to fulfilling your Dream. And so on.

Write the positive attribute for each former limitation in larger letters on the same card. Any time you feel this limitation coming on, you can return to the card and see what the positive use for that former limitation might be. Remember: it's all *your* energy. Align it toward your goal.

Be creative with this. If there are any limitations that seemingly can't be turned into assets, set them aside for now.

Turn now to the QUALITIES and ABILITIES pile. Review each quality and ability. Imagine how each quality and ability can be used to fulfill your Big Dream.

Look again at the LIMITATIONS for which you have not yet seen a positive use. What QUALITIES and ABILITIES would best help in overcoming each limitation? Let the qualities and abilities gang up—might as well let their deck be stacked in your favor; it is, after all, your deck.

Review again the cards in the *I am going to...* pile—your Big Dream and its friends. Compare each dream in that pile with your purpose. See how each fulfills that purpose perfectly.

Close your eyes, find yourself in your sanctuary, thank your Master Teacher, watch the Master Teacher disappear into the white light of the People Mover. As you turn to go, you notice a new writing on the wall of your sanctuary—your Big Dream. Except here it's not written "I am going to..." as it is on your cards.

Here it states your Big Dream, and it is simply prefaced with, "I am..."

Read it, enjoy it, become it. Move to the white light of your entryway. Bathe in it, breathe it in. Leave your sanctuary, and return to make your Dream come true.

*Take what you can use
and let the rest go by.*

KEN KESEY

Completion

By this time you should be feeling decidedly bitter-sweet. Yes, you've discovered and chosen your Big Dream, your Heart's Desire. What? No cheering? No celebration?

Not quite yet.

Lying "in the ruins" are all those other heart's de-sires—all those deserted little 3x5 cards. The reminders of the dreams that won't immediately—and might never—come true.

Sigh.

Welcome to success.

Remember that the sadness you feel is a reminder of your caring, and the caring is *your* caring—available to place behind the Big Dream you have chosen to pursue.

It is important to complete each WANT that you will not—for now—be pursuing. "Complete" doesn't mean do it; complete means declaring it done. "Complete" doesn't mean to physically finish; "complete" means *you* are complete with it—that you have completed all you're going to do about it, for now.

The down side is that you must say goodbye to a dream—maybe for good. (Whenever we say goodbye, we never really know for how long it's going to be.)

The up side is that declaring things complete frees all the mental, emotional and physical energy we've been holding in reserve for the achievement of that goal.

This can be a significant amount of energy.

For each WANT that didn't make the "I am going to..." list, and for each thing you currently have that you chose not to maintain, read it, consider it, and say, out loud, "This is complete for now." Say goodbye to it, and place it face down. Pick up another and repeat the process.

Take your time with this. You may feel the sadness, or you may feel the freeing of energy. You may cry and laugh

If you don't have enough time
to accomplish something,
consider the work finished
once it's begun.

JOHN CAGE

at the same time. Always have your Big Dream clearly in mind, so that you can direct the newly freed energy toward it.

With the freeing of the energy, you may feel that, after all, you *can* achieve this dream, too. You'll just sleep less at night, or something. This is the newly freed energy (or perhaps the comfort zone) talking. Stick to your plan. Declare it complete. Direct the energy toward the Big Dream and move on.

If the dreams you are completing involve other people, let them know you will not be doing anything more about these dreams. This is only fair. The most important person to tell, however, is yourself. This, too, is only fair.

Sometimes the "extra energy" is stored in material value. If you choose not to maintain certain physical posessions, sell them. Or, donate them. Use that good will toward your Dream. Don't wait for the things you're not maintaining to rot. Cash them in. Convert them into energy and channel that energy toward your Dream.

The amount of power freed by telling yourself you no longer choose to put energy into something can be remarkable. Be prepared for extra energy. Be prepared, as well, to channel that newly liberated energy toward your Dream.

The way to begin that is through *commitment*.

I've been on a calendar,
but I've never been on time.

MARILYN MONROE

Committing to Your Dream

Perhaps you've noticed that we haven't yet asked you to commit to your Dream. This is because, when we commit to something, *and we really mean it,* the manure hits the fan and the fan is running.

Before asking you to commit, we wanted you to understand this process, and offer some suggestions on how to use the manure as fertilizer rather than pollution.

Most people don't know much about this process, because most people don't keep most of their agreements.

Most people add a silent, unconscious modifying phrase to all their commitments: "...as long as it's not uncomfortable."

What most people don't realize is that discomfort is one of the *values* of commitments, one of the reasons for making a commitment in the first place.

Within us is an automatic goal-fulfillment mechanism. When we commit to something, we are telling the goal-fulfillment mechanism, "I want this." The goal-fulfillment mechanism says, "Fine. I'll arrange for that." And it does. Among the things it uses—individually or collectively—are:

- It looks to see what the lessons are we must learn in order to have our goal; then it arranges for those lessons. Sometimes, these lessons come in pleasant ways (we notice an article on what we need to know in a magazine; a conversation with a friend reveals something to us; a song on the radio has a line that tells us something important). At other times, the lessons are unpleasant (someone we must listen to—a boss, for example—tells us "in no uncertain terms" what we need to know; or we get sick, and the doctor tells us what we need to do "or else").

- The goal-fulfillment mechanism sees what is in the way of our having what we want, and removes it. Again, sometimes this can be pleasant (if the goal is a new car, someone offers us a great price for our

Never take a solemn oath.
People think you mean it.

NORMAN DOUGLAS

old car), or unpleasant (our car is stolen, totaled or breaks down altogether).

In order to have something new, our comfort zone must be expanded to include that new thing. The bigger the new thing, the greater the comfort zone must expand. And *comfort zones are most often expanded through discomfort.*

When people don't understand that being uncomfortable is part of the process, they use the discomfort as a reason not to do. Then they don't get what they want. We must learn to tolerate discomfort in order to grow.

This process of growth is known as "grist for the mill." When making flour in an old stone mill, it is necessary to add gravel to the wheat before grinding it. This gravel is known as *grist*. The small stones that make up the grist rub against the grain as the mill wheel passes over them. The friction causes the wheat to be ground into a fine powder. If it wasn't for the grist, the wheat would only be crushed. To grind wheat fine enough for flour requires grist. After the grinding, the grist is sifted out, and only the flour remains.

When we commit to something, the automatic goal-fulfillment mechanism throws grist in our mill. It's all designed to give us our goal.

If we don't understand the process, however, we protest, "Why are you throwing gravel in with my wheat? Stop that!" The dutiful miller uses no grist, and we wind up with crushed wheat. "This isn't what I wanted. I wanted *flour.*"

When we order flour, we must be prepared for grist in our mill. One must become an "eager learner." *Whatever* comes along, look for the lesson. *Assume* it's for your good, no matter how bad it seems.

No, there's no need to run out and *invite* disaster, just as one doesn't have to bring gravel to the mill. The necessary experiences will take place. Our job is not to *seek* them, but to *learn* from the ones that are presented to us.

*If you never want
to see a man again, say,
"I love you,
I want to marry you.
I want to have children..."
—they leave skid marks.*

RITA RUDNER

Maxwell Maltz explains the process this way: "Your automatic creative mechanism operates in terms of goals and end results. Once you give it a definite goal to achieve, you can depend on its automatic guidance system to take you to that goal much better than 'You' ever could by conscious thought. 'You' supply the goal by thinking in terms of end results. Your automatic mechanism then supplies the means whereby."

How do we know when there's grist in our mill? When we feel the comfort zone acting up, there's grist in the mill. If we discard the grist (that is, honor the comfort zone's dictates), we have crushed wheat. If we use the grist to learn the lesson at hand (that is, continue on our committed course despite the protestations of the comfort zone), we have the bouquet of flour.

Keeping agreements with others is, of course, an excellent method for getting what we want from them. If we keep our agreements, people learn to trust us. If we break our agreements, they don't. It's hard to imagine people giving something of substance to someone they don't trust.

Although people may say, "Oh, that's all right," when we make our apologies, it is seldom truly all right with people. "Unfaithfulness in keeping an appointment is an act of clear dishonesty," Horace Mann explained 150 years ago. "You may as well borrow a person's money as his time."

Although keeping agreements is a good technique for building trust with others, the real reason for keeping agreements is for building trust with *ourselves*.

If we frequently break agreements—either with another or with ourselves—we have trained ourselves to ignore our own word. So, committing to something means nothing. Committing, then, to a Big Dream is about as significant as saying we will learn to fly—sounds nice, it would be fun, but it's not going to happen.

Committing to a dream is not a one-time occurrence. It must be done daily, hourly, continually. We must *choose* to commit to our *choice,* over and over.

*The best way
to keep your word
is not to give it.*

NAPOLEON BONAPARTE

The test of this commitment is *action*. If we say, "I commit to being a great dancer," and then don't practice, that's not a commitment; that's just talk. Conversely, if we're practicing dance, we don't need to tell ourselves how committed we are. Our action *is* our demonstrated commitment.

When we commit and act, we are confronted by the comfort zone. The temptation is to stop. If we move ahead anyway—we expand the comfort zone, learn a necessary lesson, and the commitment becomes stronger. That causes us to come up against the comfort zone again, and the process continues.

Here are some suggestions for making and keeping commitments:

1. **Don't make commitments you don't plan to keep.** Some people are so casual about making agreements: "Talk to you tomorrow," "Let's get together next week," and, one of our favorites, "I'll have him call you back." You *will?* What if he doesn't want to talk to us?

   Most people like to pretend that these "casual" commitments don't count. That's not true. Every time we give our word, it counts. For the most part, most people give it entirely too often. Our word is a precious commodity and should be treated as such.

   Imagine a commitment as a precious jewel. When you give it to someone, he has the jewel. When you keep the commitment, the jewel is returned to you. If you fail to keep the agreement, however, the jewel is gone forever. (This is true of agreements with yourself as well.)

   If we hold this jewel image each time we give our word, we tend to be more careful. This image is not a metaphor, it is a reality. Our word *is* a precious jewel, and each time we give it, we risk losing it. Don't take that risk unless you plan to "cover your assets."

2. **Learn to say no.** When we commit to a Dream, one of the great tests of our sincerity is whether we

The one word you'll need is no.

BETTE DAVIS TO ROBIN WILLIAMS

say no to things not on the way to that Dream. If we commit to moving to another city, for example, temptations from the city we have not yet left appear: we're given a raise and a promotion; we hear about a larger, better, less-expensive apartment; a 24-hour gourmet restaurant (that delivers) opens; and we meet Someone Wonderful.

If we're *really* committed to moving, to all of this we must say, "No." Talk about the comfort zone acting up! Wait until Someone Wonderful calls and invites you out (or, worse, *in*) on the same evening you planned to go over the street maps of the city you plan to move to. Ouch.

Beyond this, we are programmed to feel uncomfortable saying no to people we know. We are also programmed to automatically "no" all strangers. This dual programming makes for a small circle of friends with whom we do things we don't necessarily like. To pursue a Big Dream, we must learn to say no to both programmings.

3. **Make conditional agreements.** Doctors learn to say, "I'll be there, unless I get a call from the hospital." You can, too. If there is *potentially* something more important than the agreement you are about to make, let the other person know. "I'd love to have lunch, unless I get a call-back on my audition," "I can make it, unless Greenpeace calls," or "Yes, I'll do it, if I can find a sitter for the kids." Do not, however, use this as a substitute for saying no. That turns your Big Dream into a Big Excuse and robs it of some of its power. Use the condition *only* with agreements you want to—and plan to—keep.

4. **Keep the commitments you make.** As an exercise, practice keeping *all* agreements you make—no matter how difficult, no matter how costly. This will do two things: first, it will build strength, character and inner trust. Secondly, it will get you to

*Always do sober
what you said you'd do drunk.
That will teach you to
keep your mouth shut.*

ERNEST HEMINGWAY

reread suggestions #1, #2, and #3 and follow them more carefully.

5. **Write commitments down.** Keep a calendar of some kind and write agreements down—*including agreements you make with yourself.* Don't just say, "I'm exercising tomorrow morning," write it down. Make it as important as an agreement with another.

You might want to write on a sheet of paper, "All agreements with myself shall be in writing. Everything else is just a good idea." Then place the paper somewhere you can read it—often. Eventually, there will be a difference between commitments you make with yourself and those things that would be nice, would be useful, but are not going to happen.

6. **Renegotiate at the earliest opportunity.** As soon as a possible conflict arises, contact the person with whom you have an agreement. Unless the original agreement was conditional, however, the *way* in which you renegotiate an agreement is important.

"Something more important than my agreement with you has come up," is not the best way. It's a form of breaking the agreement, just in advance. "I know I have an agreement with you, and I still plan to keep it, but something important has come up, and I wonder if we might be able to reschedule." That asks permission. If granted, you get a second chance at reclaiming your jewel. If *not* granted, see #4.

☆

And now you are ready to commit to your goal—your Dream.

It's important to commit to the fulfillment of the goal, not just to a certain amount of time spent pursuing the goal. Some people's commitments sound like this: "I'll spend two years pursuing this goal, and see what happens."

Until one is committed,
there is hesitancy,
the chance to draw back,
always ineffectiveness.
Concerning all acts
of initiative (and creation)
there is one elementary truth,
the ignorance of which kills
countless ideas and splendid plans:
that the moment
one definitely commits oneself,
then Providence moves too.
All sorts of things occur
to help one that would never
otherwise have occurred.
A whole stream of events
issues from the decision,
raising in one's favor all manner
of unforeseen incidents and meetings
and material assistance,
which no man could have dreamed
would have come his way.
I have learned a deep respect
for one of Goethe's couplets:

Whatever you can do,
or dream you can, begin it.
Boldness has genius,
power and magic in it.

W. H. MURRAY
THE SCOTTISH HIMALAYAN EXPEDITION

When we commit to *pursuing,* our goal is then *pursuing,* and we will pursue. We won't *get* what we're pursuing, because getting it is not our goal—pursuing it is.

It is fine, however, to add a time statement to your dream. When selecting a dream and making it a goal in the earlier chapter, we projected ahead five years, and then one year. You can make this any period of time you want. "I will achieve this goal within two years."

This makes it a bigger challenge, of course. We will know precisely when we have won, because we put specific parameters on the goal (so much money, a certain credential, etc.) Adding time to our goal lets us know precisely when we have *failed,* too.

This is important. To say we want something by a certain date shows us what we must do *today, right now,* to make that happen. It gets us going. If we don't achieve it, it gives us a chance to look back, see what must be done differently in the future, correct our course, recommit, and continue on.

So, add a time to your dream, and, if you so choose, commit.

The time to commit is now.

And now.

And now.

And now.

And now.

And now.

And now...

*People hate me because I am a
multifaceted, talented,
wealthy, internationally
famous genius.*

JERRY LEWIS

Keep Your Goals away from the Trolls

There is a type of crab that cannot be caught—it is agile and clever enough to get out of any crab trap. And yet, these crabs are caught by the thousands every day, thanks to a particularly human trait they possess.

The trap is a wire cage with a hole at the top. Bait is placed in the cage, and the cage is lowered into the water. One crab comes along, enters the cage, and begins munching on the bait. A second crab joins him. A third. Crab Thanksgiving. Yumm. Eventually, however, all the bait is gone.

The crabs could easily climb up the side of the cage and through the hole, but they do not. They stay in the cage. Other crabs come along and join them—long after the bait is gone. And more.

Should one of the crabs realize there is no further reason to stay in the trap and attempt to leave, the other crabs will gang up on him and stop him. They will repeatedly pull him off the side of the cage. If he is persistent, the others will tear off his claws to keep him from climbing. If he persists still, they will kill him.

The crabs—by force of the majority—stay together in the cage. The cage is hauled up, and it's dinnertime on the pier.

The chief difference between these crabs and humans is that these crabs live in water and humans on land.

Anyone who has a dream—one that might get him out of what he perceives to be a trap—had best beware of the fellow-inhabitants of the trap.

The human crabs (we call them trolls) do not usually use physical force—although they are certainly not above it. They generally don't need it, however. They have more effective methods at hand, and in mouth—innuendo, doubt, ridicule, derision, mockery, sarcasm, scorn, sneering, belittlement, humiliation, jeering, taunting, teasing, lying, and a dozen others not listed in our thesaurus.

These are the soul cages.
These are the soul cages.
Swim to the light.

STING

The way to handle such people is the same method used by Jonathan Joffrey Crab on *his* clan. (Remember that book about the crab who wasn't content to walk around, he wanted to learn underwater ballet?) Jonathan, knowing the dangers of attempted departure from the cage, said, "Hey! This is fun! What a gathering of crabs! I'm going to go get some more!" And he danced off to freedom.

Our suggestion: keep your goals away from the trolls.

People don't like to see others pursuing their dreams—it reminds them how far from living their dreams they are. In talking you out of your dreams, they are talking themselves back into their own comfort zone. They will give you every rational lie they ever gave themselves. And if you don't believe them with the same degree of devotion they do, get ready for Big Time Disapproval.

Why bother? Consider your Dream a fragile seed. It's small now, and needs protection and lots of nurturing. Eventually, it will be strong—stronger than the slings and arrows of outrageously limited people.

When you've obtained your goal, *then* tell them about it. Even though faced with irrefutable evidence, the most common expression you'll hear will be, "I don't believe it!" If they can't believe reality, imagine how much difficulty they'd have believing in your Dream.

This, of course, does not apply to close friends and supporters who have always believed in you and offer only encouragement. If you're not sure, tell them about a friend who has a similar Dream. If their response is, "Good for them!" you're in good hands. If their response is, "What a silly thing to do," it would be a silly thing, indeed, to share your goals with them.

If some people should hear of your dream and start telling you all the reasons why you can't possibly do it, you can (A) walk away, or (B) listen to them with compassion as they describe the parameters of their own comfort zones—the ones that may keep them firmly in the trap until it is hauled up.

You can have
anything you want
if you want it
desperately enough.
You must want it
with an inner exuberance
that erupts through
the skin and joins the energy
that created the world.

SHEILA GRAHAM

PART FOUR

BECOMING PASSIONATE
ABOUT YOUR DREAM

We're going to go faster. Now that you have your Dream and have committed to it, you're probably experiencing some Divine Impatience. A part of you is saying, "Let's get *on* with it!" And so we shall.

We move now from the mental realm—the world of discoveries, choices, goals and commitments—and into the emotional.

Although the mind can get the body jumping here and there, *emotion* is necessary for sustained activity. This section is about cultivating and channeling the emotional energy for consistent, persistent action.

There are a lot of different words for this emotional energy—*enthusiasm (en theos,* to be one with the energy of the divine), *desire,* and even *obsession.* The one we're, well, passionate about is *passion.*

The emotions are, however, controlled by the mind. What we *think about* determines how we *feel.* So, even though the goal is to produce passionate emotions, much of the time we'll be discussing the uses of the mind.

To reach a dream, especially a Big Dream, we need to have an ally, something to counteract all the limiting emotions the comfort zone can dish out so well.

*Put all your eggs in one basket and
WATCH THAT BASKET!*

MARK TWAIN

*Always bear in mind that your own
resolution to success is more important
than any other one thing.*

ABRAHAM LINCOLN

That thing is our passion. We must love and desire our Dream—and love and desire it *intently*—for our Dream to come true.

To paraphrase Mark Twain: "Put all your eggs in one basket—and LOVE THAT BASKET!"

Or, as Elbert Hubbard said, "Do your work with your whole heart, and you will succeed—there's so little competition."

*Losers visualize
the penalties of failure.
Winners visualize
the rewards of success.*

DR. ROB GILBERT

Visualization

To visualize is to see what is *not* there, what is *not* real—you know, a *dream*. To visualize is, in fact, to make *visual lies*.

Visual lies, however, have a way of becoming visual truths.

As we mentioned earlier, don't let the word *visual* throw you. We're talking about the imagination. Some people primarily *see* things in their imagination. Others primarily *feel* things. Still others primarily *hear* things. Whichever sense you use to access your imagination is fine.

How do you visualize? What does it look (feel, sound) like? The same way you remember things, that's how the imagination looks-feels-sounds. What's the shape of an apple? What color is a carrot? ("Why is a carrot more orange than an orange?" asked the Amboy Dukes. That was back in the sixties. You had to be there.) What is your bathroom sink like? How clean is your car? However you saw or sensed or heard those images, that's what it's like to *visualize* the future in your imagination.

But you know all this. You already have a sanctuary built in your imagination, and probably a few taco stands, too. With such advanced readers, it must be time for a *Pop Quiz!* (Take a deep breath, now.)

POP QUIZ: Although the brain is only 2% of the total body weight, it consumes 25% of the body's oxygen. What does this mean?

(A) If you feel short of breath, stop thinking.
(B) People without brains need 25% less oxygen.
(C) Our brains should be bigger.
(D) The body considers thinking an important activity.
(E) We should spend 75% of our time doing something other than thinking.
(F) You shouldn't walk, think and chew gum at the same time.
(G) Keep breathing.

In our imagination, what we behold we become. What we have beheld until this moment has gotten us what we

Never give in.
Never. Never. Never. Never.

WINSTON CHURCHILL

are—and what we *have*. If we want something different—something greater—we must think greater thoughts.

We are not responsible for every thought that goes wandering through our mind. We *are,* however, responsible for the ones we *hold* there. We're *especially* responsible for the thoughts we *put* there.

It's time to plant a Dream crop of positive visions. It's time to focus on the positive; to hold an image of what we want; to see, view, play *(s'il vous plait)* our Dream.

Or, worded for our more negatively thinking friends: Don't focus on what you don't want.

Think about your Dream *all the time,* no matter what else you're doing. Live your Dream in your imagination. Become obsessed by it. Love it. Be passionate about it.

To paraphrase Churchill: Never lose in your imagination. Never. Never. Never. Never.

It's *your* dream. *Your* imagination. Why on earth should you lose? Don't. If you find yourself losing, turn it around. Call in a calvary charge. Bring on the Tooth Fairy. Whatever it takes.

Always come out on top, always be victorious. Always win.

I used to work at
The International House
of Pancakes.
It was a dream,
and I made it happen.

PAULA POUNDSTONE

Affirmations

To affirm is to make firm. An affirmation is a statement of truth you make firm by repetition.

Affirmations always take place in the present, hence the wording is always present tense. *"I am* a successful orchestral conductor, making $100,000 per year," is how to state an affirmation, not, "I'm going to be..." or "I really want to be..." or "If it's not too much trouble, I'd really like to be..."

Make an affirmation for

- Your purpose
- Your Big Dream
- Each of the goals along the path to the Big Dream

Read each affirmation out loud *at least* 1,000 times. (An hour each for your Purpose and Big Dream; 30 minutes each for your other goals.) Before starting, ask the white light to surround you for your highest good.

When you affirm, all that is between you and fulfilling that dream surfaces—in other words, the gunk of comfort zone. Expect fear, guilt, unworthiness, hurt feelings, anger and discouragement to do what they do to get you to stop.

Keep going.

To bring up the limitations faster, look at yourself in the mirror while repeating your affirmation out loud.

You can record your affirmations on an endless-loop cassette (the kind used for outgoing messages in answering machines) and play it softly in the background no matter what else is going on.

You can get an earphone and play your tape on a portable stereo wherever you go. Talk about your portable paradise.

You can put your affirmations on the walls of your sanctuary so that you see them every time you come in.

*The thing always happens
that you really believe in;
and the belief in a thing
makes it happen.*

FRANK LLOYD WRIGHT

Some people like to make a Treasure Map. A treasure map is a large piece of paper—or bulletin board—that contains the path to your inner and outer treasure. Cut from magazines, newspapers, etc. things that represent portions of your Big Dream—words, pictures, people, anything.

Glue, paste or pin them to your treasure map. (Some people use a bulletin board so that when one portion of the Dream comes true, they can take it down and replace it with the next part of the Dream.) It becomes a colorful collage. Put it where you'll see it often (but not where the trolls hang out). It's a visual affirmation.

Practice turning any of the comfort zone's *negative* affirmations into instant affirmations. Anytime you catch yourself saying negative things to yourself, take charge of the thought and rescue it. Turn it around. Make the most negative thought the most positive one, just like that. Consider it a lesson in creative writing, or a new quiz show—the grand prize of which is your Dream. If stuck, you can always add, "...up until now, and things are changing for the better," to whatever negative nonsense the comfort zone throws at you.

Affirmations help you believe in your Dream. Belief is essential. Your Dream must become more real than your doubt. Affirmations are like lifting weights—a mechanical process that helps build strength (belief) in your Dream.

"One person with belief," John Stewart Mill wrote more than a hundred years ago, "is equal to a force of ninety-nine who have only interests."

If you want a quality,
act as if you already had it.
Try the "as if" technique.

WILLIAM JAMES

A Place to Practice Success

We bet you already know the place we're going to suggest. Yes, the pool hall. No. Your *sanctuary*.

All the tools of the sanctuary—the Light at the Entryway, the Main Room, the People Mover, the Information Retrieval System, the Video Screen, the Ability Suits, the Ability Suit Practice Area, the Health Center, the Playroom, the Sacred Room, and the Master Teacher—are invaluable tools in visualizing and affirming your Dream.

Think of all the experts—past, present and future—you can invite in on the People Mover. ("Mark Twain told me today, 'Courage is the mastery of fear—not absence of fear.'" Amaze your friends!)

Think of how much fun you can have wearing the Ability Suit of your Dream in the Ability Suit Practice Area. If that becomes too vigorous, you can sit down and *watch* yourself being successful on the Video Screen. The Information Retrieval System is the perfect place to go whenever you think, "I wish I knew about..."

And, of course, there's the Master Teacher. What a friend, guide, supporter, fellow-traveler, champion and *bon vivant*.

All this—and so much more—is only the close of an eyelid away. Use it. Often.

Have I ever told you you're my hero?
You're everything I would like to be.
I can climb higher than an eagle.
You are the wind beneath my wings.

LARRY HENLEY

JEFF SILBAR

Find a Hero

We all need a hero, a role model—someone who had a Dream as big as ours, and lived it.

Your hero may be alive, or may "belong to the ages." Either way, he or she can live in your heart.

Kevin Kline met his hero, Sir John Gielgud. Kline was in awe. "Mr. Gielgud," he said, "Do you have any advice for a young actor about to make his first film in London?"

Gielgud stopped and pondered the question for some time. At last he spoke, "The really good restaurants are in Chelsea and the outlying regions—you want to avoid the restaurants in the big hotels."

Pianist Vladimir Horowitz asked the advice of the great conductor Arturo Toscanini. "If you want to please the critics," Toscanini told him, "don't play too loud, too soft, too fast, too slow."

"Meet the sun every morning as if it could cast a ballot," Henry Cabot Lodge, Jr. told novice political campaigner Dwight D. Eisenhower. A few years later, President Eisenhower met another of his heroes, golfer Sam Snead. When Eisenhower asked him for some advice on how to improve his golf swing, Snead coached, "Put your ass into the ball, Mr. President!"

Eisenhower himself became a hero to millions. "This must have been how Eisenhower felt just before D-Day," Larry Appleton explained to Balki Bartoukomous. "All around him the troops sleeping; not Ike! He knew that one single mistake could change the course of world history." Balki had only one question: "Was this before or after Ike met Tina Turner?"

A young George Gershwin came to the already famous Irving Berlin, looking for a job as piano player. After hearing some of Gershwin's music, Berlin refused to hire Gershwin. "What the hell do you want to work for somebody else for?" Berlin asked, "Work for yourself!"

The one thing I do not want
to be called is First Lady.
It sounds like a saddle horse.

JACQUELINE KENNEDY

I wish I was Donna Reed—
she'd have something wonderful to say.
...Or Shirley Jones—
she'd have something wonderful to say, too,
and maybe even some fresh-baked cookies...
Or Loretta Young;
of course, she wouldn't have anything
wonderful to say, but she would make
a stunning entrance.

JESSICA TATE

A playwright asked his hero, George Bernard Shaw, if he should continue with the profession of playwrighting. "Go on writing plays, my boy," Shaw encouraged, "One of these days one of these London producers will go into his office and say to his secretary, 'Is there a play from Shaw this morning?' and when she says, 'No,' he will say, 'Well, then we'll have a start on the rubbish.' And that's your chance, my boy."

Heroes don't have to be real. Some find fictional characters more inspiring than real-life heroes. To this day, thousands of people write to Sherlock Holmes at 221-B Baker Street. There is currently a bank at that address. It dutifully responds to every letter, "Mr. Holmes thanks you for your letter. At the moment he is in retirement in Sussex, keeping bees."

One of the nicest things about heroes is they were *human*. There's hardly a hero you can name who didn't have heroic flaws. (Even Holmes had his weaknesses—that seven-percent solution of cocaine, for example.) Judy Garland once said of another singer, "The first time I saw her perform she was so good I wanted to run up to the stage, put my arms around her—and wring her neck. She just has too much talent!"

When we realize that our heroes became heroes *flaws and all,* it gives us hope. "You mean we don't have to be perfect to fulfill our Dream, to make a contribution?" Hardly.

It takes commitment, courage and passion to live a dream and make a contribution. Heroes had these qualities *along with* their flaws. And you have those qualities, too.

And, of course, when you find one, go visit your hero often in your sanctuary.

I was going to buy a copy of
The Power of Positive Thinking,
and then I thought:
What the hell good
would that do?

RONNIE SHAKES

MARY RICHARDS: It's a lousy business
we're in, Mr. Grant; I quit.
I'm going to Africa
to work with Schweitzer.
LOU GRANT: Mary,
Albert Schweitzer is dead.
MARY RICHARDS: You see what I mean,
Mr. Grant? It's a lousy, lousy world.

THE MARY TYLER MOORE SHOW

Positive Focusing vs. Positive Thinking

There is a myth that in order to reach our goal we must "think positive" all the time. No, we don't have to "think positive" all the time. We don't even have to think positive*ly* all the time.

To succeed—to fulfill our dream—all we have to do is keep focused on our goal and keep moving toward it.

Let's say person A, person B and person C all set out for the same goal. They begin at the same place at the same time. Person A is a positive thinker, person B is a positive focuser, person C is both a positive thinker *and* a positive focuser.

At the "Go," person A decides to sit down and do a little positive thinking to help prepare for the journey. Person B focuses on the goal and gets moving. Person C gets moving, too.

Person A notices an area of unpositiveness within, and continues to sit, working hard to remove the "darkness" before moving on the journey. Person B does not like the road, does not like the rules, does not like the weather, does not like the planned lunch, etc., but keeps moving toward the goal nonetheless. Person C keeps moving, too, while enjoying the flowers, waving at passersby, singing, and thinking what good exercise all this movement is.

Guess who gets to the goal first? It's a tie between B and C. Person A hasn't left the starting place—but is feeling much more positive than before, thank you very much. If person B and person C arrived at the goal at the same time, then what was the point of all that positive focusing? Why bother?

Person C *enjoyed* the journey, person B did not. That's the only difference. As long as we stay focused on our goal and continue moving toward it, we can have all the negative thoughts we want.

*Keep walking
and keep smiling.*

TINY TIM

In terms of goals, what's the difference? Well, if we were to ask C, "How would you like to go toward another goal?" C might respond, "Sure. That was fun." Person B, on the other hand, might reply, "I worked hard to get here. I want to rest for a while. Enjoy my victory."

What's the point? There are two. First, if your thoughts are not always sweetness and light as you move toward your dream, don't worry. If you keep moving, you'll still get to your Dream.

Second, as you move toward your goal, you might like to practice focusing on the positive along the way. You don't have to "make something up"—you already have; it's called your Big Dream. You need only look at *what's in front of you* and *find something there to appreciate*.

Our lives are a combination of good and bad, positive and negative. It's the best of times and the worst of times, all the time. When we focus on the good *that's already present,* we feel better. If not, we don't. Either way, life goes on.

Keeping your mind on the goal and moving toward the goal is the essence of positive focusing. All the rest is fun, but not essential.

Unless, of course, you consider fun to be essential.

*Creativity can solve
almost any problem.
The creative act,
the defeat of habit
by originality,
overcomes everything.*

GEORGE LOIS

The Energy of Achievement

In the East, the movement of energy in the human body is studied and charted as meticulously as the movement of, say, bodily fluids are studied and charted in the West.

As the merging of East and West continues, the wisdoms of each are being explored and incorporated by the other. Some Eastern health practitioners now have circulation charts on their walls, and some Western doctors have charts indicating the meridians of the body and acupressure points.

We're going to talk about the movement of one kind of energy within the body—the energy of achievement. There are other energies, of course, just as there are fluids other than blood. We're discussing the energy of achievement because it relates most directly to manifestation—toward making our dreams come true.

This is the energy of individual creation. It's quite powerful. It is also experienced as sexual energy (recreative or procreative) and as spiritual energy. (This is the spiritual energy as it is perceived *within* the body. To the degree that there is spiritual energy *outside* the body— and how that might be organized and tapped—is a matter of speculation and belief we shall leave to the Gap.)

People experience achievement energy differently depending on what they call it. Just as a certain energy in the body can be called "fear" or "excitement," so, too, the energy of achievement can be called creative, sexual or spiritual.

This energy is produced in the body in an area that extends from about the navel to approximately mid-thigh. It extends in a band, all the way around the body. The center of it is the area known in Western anatomy as the *perineum*. To quote The American Heritage: "The region between the scrotum and the anus in males, and between the posterior vulva junction and the anus in females."

*Creative activity could be
described as a type of learning
process where teacher and
pupil are located
in the same individual.*

ARTHUR KOESTLER

Even reading a dictionary definition of the location of this center of energy is enough to activate most people's comfort zones. As we'll see shortly, this is precisely why this energy is not available as fully as it could be. For now, allow your comfort zone to do what it does, and read on.

The energy of achievement is designed to move up, toward the brain, where the mind directs it. ("Wash the car." "Fix dinner." "Write a Pulitzer Prize-winning novel.") The mind is like the rudder of a ship—with small motions, it guides the powerful ship in the direction set by the captain (you).

Here's an ideal scene of how this energy moves within the body. The energy moves up, into the area of the stomach—a circular area with the navel at its center. Here it picks up *excitement* and more *power*—the power to make changes. It rises further, to the solar plexus. Here, the energy becomes more focused and takes on a *solid, grounded, reliable* quality. The energy travels higher, to the center of the chest, where it acquires *loving* and *caring*. This excited, powerful, focused, solid, grounded, reliable, loving and caring energy (we call it *passion*) presents itself to the mind, asking, "What shall we do?"

The process can go the other way, too. The mind may have a direction—a task—and send down for some energy. "Coming right up!" the creative energy responds, and rises to the occasion.

With this free flow of energy, directed toward a goal, it's easy to see how seemingly effortless the fulfillment of dreams can be. It actually sounds like *fun.*

Not many people, however, experience it in this way. What happened? If we overlay the comfort zone, and the misperceptions we were programmed to have as to the use of various emotions, the answer is obvious.

The energy begins to rise from the creative center. Because it's coming from "down there," we immediately begin to wonder, "What's wrong?" Most of us were trained that any sensations from "down there" involves either elimination or sexuality—two things that are icky at best

Excuse me,
I have to use the toilet.
Actually, I have to use
the telephone,
but I'm too embarrassed
to say so.

DOROTHY PARKER

and forbidden at worst. One then feels either fearful or guilty, or—usually—both.

If the sensation is some form of elimination, for many the first thought is, "Can this be postponed?" There is a great deal of fear connected with elimination—fear of germs, fear of pain, fear of touching anything icky, fear of terrible smells. (Actually, people don't much mind their own smells, but if someone else were to smell them—disaster!) Many people are embarrassed (another word for fearful) about elimination. There are almost as many euphemisms for elimination as there are for death—going to the rest room (what are you going to rest?), the powder room (what is there to powder?), the bathroom (you're going to take a *bath?*), and so on.

If the energy is perceived as sexual, the almost automatic response of most people is, "How do I get rid of this?" It is treated as some sort of *irritation*.

For some, fear and guilt *insist* that the energy be overcome, suppressed, crushed, "put down," and subdued. If this sounds like the response of a military dictator to a people's revolt, it is not coincidental. This energy, according to some people's training, is to be neither experienced nor expressed. Some pull God into it at this point, telling themselves that fear and guilt are really Direct Messages from the Almighty. It's not "moral" to feel these feelings, they tell themselves. What was a simple revolution becomes a battle for one's Immortal Soul.

For others—many who consider themselves "sexually liberated"—the desire to eliminate any sexual feelings is just as strong. They, however, use *action* rather than *suppression*.

When the creative energies begin to rise and are perceived as sexual, one is, in the popular terminology, *horny*. Horny does not mean, "Oh, I'm going to spend loving, tender, intimate moments with the one I love." Horny means, "How can I get rid of this energy?" *Satisfaction* is defined as what you feel *after* this energy is released. Through promiscuous sexual activity—with self or with others—it is. The feeling behind all this is *fear*—fear that it will get

*I'm at an age where I think
more about food than sex.
Last week I put a mirror over
my dining room table.*

RODNEY DANGERFIELD

worse, as though sexual feelings were some sort of *curse*, that if they become great enough someone might *explode*.

Both suppression and promiscuity are based upon the same thing—a deeply seated cultural taboo against sex. Yes, sex is everywhere in our culture, but it's everywhere *because* of the taboo. This is especially true of humor, which is a great barometer of what is forbidden and what is accepted by a culture. Jokes about things forbidden are automatically funnier than jokes about things accepted.

"But sex is a natural function. Wouldn't it be joked about because of that?" Moving the blood through our body is a natural function, too, but how many jokes are there circulating about blood flow? Without the sexual taboo, jokes about sex wouldn't be as titillating.

We *look* for sex jokes. We even have a special term for puns of a sexual nature—*double entendre* (borrowed from the French, of course). ("I am now going to attempt," Bette Midler told her audience as a drum roll flourished, "my world-famous *quadruple* entendre!") For example, in the last paragraph, there was a sexual pun and a biological pun. Did you notice one or both? Which is funny (in a juvenile sort of way) and which is just mildly interesting (in a linguistic fashion)? (The puns, by the way, were in the words *circulate* and *titillate.*)

The result of this sexual taboo is *guilt*. We feel something we shouldn't be feeling—that *nobody* should be feeling—and we feel guilty. Rather than explore the underlying belief and accept that having sexual energy is *not* "bad," most people either suppress the feeling, or rebel *against* the guilt, and act upon the sexual feeling promiscuously. Either action is a reaction to the guilt.

The confusion this can cause when the energy is being used creatively or spiritually is obvious. One may be involved in a creative project. The creative energy is flowing more and more. Then, for a moment, it is interpreted as sexual. "Oh, dear," the creating person says, "I'd better do something about this," and moves into his or her habitual response to sexual energy. Be that suppression or expression, the use of the energy in a creative way is stopped.

Creativity represents a miraculous coming together of the uninhibited energy of the child with its apparent opposite and enemy, the sense of order imposed on the disciplined adult intelligence.

NORMAN PODHORETZ

The same happens when people are involved in spiritual practices—prayer, meditation, contemplation, spiritual exercises—and the spiritual energy begins flowing. When experienced for a moment as sexual, the same turmoil about "what-to-do-about-sex" takes over, and the spiritual heights to which one can ride this energy are not reached.

When this energy is needed for creative or spiritual work, it's obvious that to eliminate it—through suppression or expression—before it has a chance to get beyond the fear and guilt of the stomach, is, shall we say, not productive.

We are not advocating increased sexual activity for the suppressors, nor are we advocating celibacy for the expressers. We are suggesting that the sexual energy be considered a *welcome* energy in the body. It is not bad. It does not have to be suppressed or eliminated. Allowing it to simply *be there* forms the basis for one to choose *how* this energy will be used. In any given moment, that choice may be to use it creatively, spiritually or sexually. When we're "on automatic" about the sexual energy, we cannot choose.

Let's say the energy makes it past the stomach. It has gained excitement (rather than fear) and power to change (rather than guilt). The next hurdle is unworthiness. This is a formidable one. "Who do you think you are to have this kind of energy? And just what do you plan to do with it, anyway?"

These are significant questions. Even if a person has pondered them intellectually and arrived at a satisfactory conclusion, seldom is that conclusion grounded so fully in the body that it automatically answers, "I am me, this is my energy, and I'm using it to fulfill my Dream." (If used as spiritual energy, the response might be, "This is God's energy, and I'm using it to do God's work.")

Unworthiness's only response to this is, "Oh, right, you may pass. And here's some solid, grounded, reliable energy to take with you."

You've got to create a dream.
You've got to
uphold the dream.
If you can't,
go back to the factory
or go back to the desk.

ERIC BURDON

Unworthiness stands as a gatekeeper. It has an important job: let only a certain amount of energy pass for a certain task. As we discussed before, most people, unfortunately, have unworthiness programmed to allow almost *nothing* to pass—they are unworthy of all things, certainly all things *new*.

Visualizations, affirmations, sanctuary work, and so on, give unworthiness new instructions. "It is all right to let energy for the fulfillment of this Dream pass. In addition, you are to add *to* this energy some of your solid, grounded, reliable energy."

When the energy gets above unworthiness, it comes upon the third checkpoint. There it often finds a wounded heart.

Most people, over time, have developed a definite attitude toward emotional hurt: "I'm never going to let that happen to me again." The misperception is that it was the *loving* and the *caring* that caused the hurt, "And if I never love or care about anything ever again, I won't be hurt."

This is the I-may-never-win-but-at-least-I'll-never-lose attitude we discussed earlier. It is a decision made in early childhood, and the limited logic and perception of a child is the "rule" with which many people govern their adult lives.

To this rule, the energy of achievement is a major threat. "This Dream you're going after—it's a *risk*. We might *fail*. That would hurt, and I can't stand being hurt anymore. You can't pass." If pressed (by now the energy is fairly powerful), the anger that often covers the hurt arises and says, "I *said* no. I *mean* no. Now leave me *alone*."

When the heart is taught, with gentleness and affection, that risk is a part of winning, and that hurt is a part of caring, and that hurt heals, it can allow the energy to pass. And the heart, of course, being the heart, automatically adds loving and caring to the energy as it moves through.

*Any activity becomes creative
when the doer cares about
doing it right, or better.*

JOHN UPDIKE

At that moment, the heart thrills. In giving, it is reborn. It comes alive. It has something—the Dream—to love again—and loving is its nature, its very life. And the wounds of the past begin to heal. The wounds are forgiven, and, as importantly, forgotten.

If all this energy gets to an unfocused mind, of course, it's all dissipated. The energy is scattered here and scattered there. The power to fulfill a Dream is lost. That's why we've spent so much time in this book on the significance of the Dream—the importance of knowing the specific direction toward which the ship is to be steered.

This is what happens when the energy begins in the creative center and rises to the mind. When the mind sends its request down for some achievement energy to fulfill a given project, it's easy to see how the mind's request might never make contact with the very energy it seeks to petition.

The first challenge the mind faces is the wounded heart. It seldom gets beyond it. "We've been hurt too many times by your bright ideas. Go away." The mind returns to its station, where yet another "best laid plan" remains unfulfilled.

This is why most people have so many wants, desires and "good ideas" bouncing around in their heads—they never got them past the hurt feelings (and its close friend, anger). This is why the excuses many people have for not living their dreams are so filled with *blame.* "I would have done it, except so-and-so let me down," or "...so-and-so *would have* let me down."

If the idea *does* get through the heart, it gathers the caring energy and moves on. Until it comes upon unworthiness. "You can't have it *just now.* You're not good enough *just yet.* Come back *later."*

This is why so many projects we *really loved* failed. Unworthiness is subtle in its sabotage. One of its key weapons is "Later." The concept of "later" makes sense to the mind—it's logical. Not everything can be done all at

*The essential conditions
of everything you do must be
choice, love, passion.*

NADIA BOULANGER

once. The mind buys this, and returns to the brain to wait. (We'll talk more about *later*—later.)

If the mind does move through unworthiness (often with the anger of the heart saying, "Enough with the laters, already!") it enters the land of fear and guilt. Here, one logical-sounding reason after another is given for why nothing should ever change in any way. Fear and guilt know how to cite scripture and verse—either from a book, a movie, a TV show, a newspaper, or from one's own life— as *proof* that the proposed idea is unworkable, preposterous and downright *dangerous*.

The mind, dazzled by this seemingly *factual* presentation, goes "home" to think. It tries to discover a less dangerous way. Alas, fear and guilt shoot down every idea the mind formulates with even more logic than the last time. (The fact that some of the new logic *contradicts* the logic of last time is not always noticed.) And so the mind is left alone—pondering.

☆

All these energies are part of the *success mechanism* we have as human beings. That this mechanism has been misdirected and incorrectly programmed (for adults, at least) does not in any way affect the *usefulness* of the structure. (It is, in fact, doing a very good job at what it was programmed to do.)

Please remember: the goal is not to "get rid of" any part of this mechanism. The goal is to redirect and reprogram it so that it achieves what *we* choose—not the choices made for us by parents, teachers and society when we were too young to make choices of our own.

*Every creator painfully
experiences the chasm between
his inner vision and its
ultimate expression.*

ISAAC BASHEVIS SINGER

Liberating Achievement Energy

The various blockages to the free flow of achievement energy prevent us from directing all our available energy toward our Dream. The energy is "damned" up inside ("damn this," "damn that").

We know the names of those blockages—they are our comfort-zone buddies: fear, guilt, unworthiness, hurt feelings and anger. Each of these limitations has two aspects—a psychological (or mental) one, and a physiological (or physical) one.

The psychological aspect—and how to reprogram it with visualizations, affirmations, etc.—we've explored in other chapters. In this chapter, we're going to suggest some ways in which this energy can be *physiologically* freed.

As we mentioned before, each of the comfort zone's limitations has a favorite place to gather in the body—fear and guilt prefer the stomach, unworthiness the solar plexus, hurt feelings and anger the chest. It was the *mind* and its *thoughts,* of course, that created these limitations in the first place. The limitations have, however, been "living" in a certain part of the body for so long, that that part of the body has *physically* taken on the attributes of that limitation.

We know, for example, that mental stress ("pressure") can create tension in the neck and shoulders. In some people, however, that mental stress has been so constant and unrelenting, that they have tension in the neck and shoulders *all the time*—even when they're *not* under stress. It's known as *chronic tension.*

The same is true of fear, guilt, unworthiness, hurt feelings and anger. We tend to have *chronic* limitations built into the structure of our body. This is why—even when everything is going great—we can feel "free floating" fear, guilt, unworthiness, hurt or anger.

The comfort zone, then, is "built into" our body.

*Take a music bath once or
twice a week for a few seasons,
and you will find that
it is to the soul what
the water-bath is to the body.*

OLIVER WENDELL HOLMES

That is, of course, bad news. No matter how much "mental" work we do, there is the physical tension in our body that will counteract it. The *good* news is that, being physical, we can reduce these physical tensions through *physical* means.

The good news continued: The techniques for removing tensions in the body are varied, plentiful and, for the most part, pleasurable. The last thirty years have seen a rebirth of these techniques in the West. These include massage, stretching, breathing, exercise, touching ("laying on of hands")—and the old standby, hot baths. Entire schools are devoted to the study of just one form of tension relief—and there are dozens of these schools.

We are not going to explore all of them in this chapter. (We want this book to be the size of a *regular* book, not a *telephone* book.) We will, however, mention a few. Know that *any* technique that relieves physical tension can be used to reduce the chronic physical tension of fear, guilt, unworthiness, hurt feelings and anger.

Before suggesting any techniques, there is one thing to keep in mind about physical stress release: When the stress is released, it is usually reexperienced. If you've ever had your shoulders rubbed, you probably noticed that, for a while, they hurt *more* as they were being massaged. Along with this hurt was probably a good feeling—one of release. This is often referred to as, "It hurts so good."

The same is true of fear, guilt, unworthiness, hurt feelings and anger. As each is released, the feeling itself may intensify. But along with the intensity comes the good feeling of release. Often, that good feeling is the *other* quality of the limitation—excitement for fear, power of personal change for guilt, worthiness for unworthiness, caring for hurt feelings, and power for external change for anger.

In all cases, know that if the feeling you want to reduce, in fact, *intensifies*—that's part of the process. To the degree you can, focus on the *good* feeling that accompanies it.

*I've got to keep breathing.
It'll be my worst business
mistake if I don't.*

SIR NATHAN MEYER ROTHSCHILD

Breathing and Stretching: It's hard to tell which of the techniques for removing physical tension is the oldest, but we'd put our chips on breathing and stretching. A great many animals further down the evolutionary ladder take deep breaths and stretch for the same reasons humans do—it relieves tension, and it feels good.

Breathing increases the supply of oxygen to the body. Stretching moves that oxygen around (through increased blood flow to the area being stretched). Fortunately, we can consciously breathe into, and, by breathing into it, stretch each of the comfort zone's strongholds—the stomach, the solar plexus and the chest.

Try breathing into each of these places, consciously expanding the area as you do so. If you like, as you breathe in, you can imagine a white light going to that area. As you breathe out, you can imagine any darkness (tension) that was in the area expelled with the exhale.

Breathing deeply into an area of tension can be done anywhere, anytime. You can practice it "formally," lying down (it's sometimes nice to place your hands over the area you're breathing into), or, it can be used whenever and wherever the comfort zone wishes to remind you that "you can't have what you want."

Stretching through movement is a great way to break up the comfort zone's patterning. Leaning back—supporting yourself with your hands on your lower back—stretches all the areas at once. So does lying on the floor, face down, and arching your back by pushing the top part of your body off the floor with your hands.

You probably cannot touch your elbows together behind your back, but if you *attempt* it, it stretches the heart center. If you lean slightly back while doing that, it stretches the solar plexus and stomach as well.

Physical Exercise: Using the muscles in the area of a limitation can help break up the limitation. Does this mean people with washboard stomachs have no fear? Not necessarily. (Although they obviously have no fear of

I like long walks,
especially when they are taken
by people who annoy me.

FRED ALLEN

exercise.) There is, however, a definite zone-busting effect to increasing blood flow into an area.

Hot Baths: Is all that exercise too strenuous for you? Here's a stress-reduction technique designed in heaven—the hot bath. Alas, many of us don't take hot baths very often. We live in a "shower power" culture. Maybe if you considered them *therapeutic,* you can find more time for them. There are few things that release general physical tension better.

Touch: Simply placing your hands on the areas of limitation can have profound results. It is usually best against bare skin, but through clothing works, too. You can imagine a white light flowing through your hands, into the area, releasing the tension. This is especially useful if combined with breathing. Touching yourself is something you can do *almost* anywhere. (Some people have become experts at doing it casually in public, as though it were the most natural thing in the world—which it is. Others pretend to be doing something else, such as gently scratching an itch.) A touch can send a message to a disturbed area, "Peace. Be still."

Massage: Not only can we *breathe* into each of the areas favored by the comfort zone, we can also reach each of them with *both* our hands. (Is this luck, or just good design? That might be a question for the Gap.) Physically manipulating the stomach, solar plexus and chest is an excellent way to break up the patterns of limitation residing there. The process is made even more effective (and, dare we say, *enjoyable)* with the addition of massage oil.

It's also good to get professionally massaged. Let the masseur or masseuse know the areas you'd like to work on in particular. You can also tell him or her which limitations you're seeking to reduce. He or she may have some additional techniques specific to a given school of massage.

☆

*An Englishman thinks he is
moral when he is only
uncomfortable.*

GEORGE BERNARD SHAW

Any of these techniques are made more powerful when combined with *mental* work. Imagining a Dream while eliminating a barrier to that Dream can have profound effects.

What you're doing in these situations is reducing a limitation in *both* its abodes—mentally *and* physically. When a limitation is tossed out of both its thriving places often enough, it might just move back to the Midwest where it came from. (Or, perhaps, New England. As Cleveland Amory pointed out, "The New England conscience doesn't keep you from doing what you shouldn't—it just keeps you from enjoying it.")

Speaking of enjoying it, all these techniques do have within them an element of physical pleasure. In addition to enjoying it, *use* it, too. Allow yourself to *feel good*—physically—about your Dream. So often our dreams have been accompanied by physically feeling bad (thanks to the comfort zone).

More on this in the next chapter. For now, know that time spent doing body work is time well invested. Both benefits are significant—less hold of the comfort zone, and more creative energy to pursue your Dream.

*Success is not the result
of spontaneous combustion.
You must set yourself on fire.*

REGGIE LEACH

Redirecting Energies

When we discuss being *passionate* about a dream, many people think, "Passion? Passion is supposed to be for..." They then name the thing they happen to be passionate about (or feel guilty about doing all the time, which they do because of passion—passion *is* stronger than guilt).

Most people have their passion hard-wired (and often hot-wired) toward a particular thing. It might be a person, certain foods, a given TV program, sex, money, football, macrame—whatever. The list of things people feel passionate about is almost as long as a list of things.

What we feel passionate about is our choice. For most of us, however, the choice was made long ago, and we forgot that we chose. We *know* what the choice *is*—the thing we automatically feel passionate about—but we've forgotten having made the choice.

As we free the achievement energy within ourselves, it will naturally flow toward what we already feel passionate about. It's "wired" that way. It's the path of least resistance inside. If that's already your goal, great. If it is something *other* than your goal, that newly liberated energy can be redirected.

Notice we said "newly liberated." We're not suggesting you feel any *less* passionate about the things you currently feel passionate for—unless those things are not part of your Dream.

We're saying that most of us have a lot more passion than we currently allow ourselves to feel. As we feel this energy more, give of the *overflow* to your Dream. That overflow may be ten times what is currently felt, but give of it anyway. Your Dream requires—and deserves—a lot of energy.

In general, passion is "wired" to a particular thing through *thoughts*. We think about something, we feel passion; we feel passion, we think about something more;

*Passion is in all great
searches and is necessary
to all creative endeavors.*

W. EUGENE SMITH

we think about something more, we feel more passion. It's an expanding cycle. Like the chicken-and-egg puzzlement, it's hard to tell which came first.

Also like the chicken-and-egg puzzlement, it doesn't matter. We have chickens, we have eggs—that's all that matters. We have passion, we have things we feel passionate about—that's what matters.

You can, then, redirect the passion from something you currently feel passionate about, to your Dream, at any point in the cycle. All it takes is (A) remembering to do it, and (B) a *specific* image to feel passionate about.

Specific images are important. A general image of a Dream ("I want to be a movie star") is too vague. It doesn't have enough, uh, *fascination* to pull the passion from the current object of desire.

For someone whose dream is being a movie star, a specific image might be winning an Oscar. What *specifically* about winning an Oscar turns you on the most? Is it the moment you hear your name announced? Is it the moment you are being patted on the back by all those around you, and giving an obligatory kiss to your companion, whoever that may be? Maybe it's standing at the podium, bright lights shining down on you, slightly out of breath, listening to the ovation, Oscar in your hand, remembering Barbra Streisand's comment on winning her Oscar, "Hello, gorgeous!"

These are *specific* images. If you are doing some of your body work and releasing one of the limiting emotions, if this also releases some passion, then direct that passion toward the specific image of your Big Dream. If you're thinking passionately about whatever you currently find passionating (as we said, what would a self-help book be without a coined word or two—this was number two), direct that passion toward the specific image.

As an exercise, find a specific image of your Dream. Say, winning the Oscar. Now, close your eyes and think about something—not directly related to your Dream—that you tend to feel passionate about. Let's say it's

*Many persons have
a wrong idea of what
constitutes true happiness.
It is not attained through
self-gratification but through
fidelity to a worthy purpose.*

HELEN KELLER

chocolate cake. Think about chocolate cake. Think about how good it tastes. In your imagination, see it, smell it, taste it—let the juices (and the passion) flow.

Then, *snap,* place in your mind the image of the Oscar. Let the passion built by and for chocolate cake be directed at golden Oscar. If cake comes back in (and it will), let it. ("Let them think cake.") Let the passion build again, then, *snap,* switch to Oscar.

At first, you probably won't be able to hold the specific image for long. The mind will go back to what it habitually feels passionate about. This is what we meant by "hard-wired." With practice, however, transferring passion from one object to another becomes easier and easier. Eventually, when you feel passion stirring in your body, it will *automatically* move toward your Dream.

As an advanced exercise, switch the thought from The Passionate Thing to the specific image *while doing the passionate thing.* No, this is not an excuse to go have some chocolate cake. ("I ate an entire chocolate cake last night—it's an exercise in a book I'm reading.") Although we couldn't imagine anything that would sell more copies of our book, we must suggest you don't do The Passionate Thing just for the purposes of this exercise.

The next time you *are* doing The Passionate Thing, however, from time to time, mentally switch to your specific image. (If it involves another person, *do* be discreet. "What are you doing?" "I'm sorry, dear, I was thinking about an Oscar." "Oscar who?!")

Yes, you *can* have your cake, and think about your next bestseller, too. *We* do it all the time!

Sometimes I sits and thinks
and sometimes I just sits.

Meditate, Contemplate or Just Sits

In addition to visualization, you might like to try any number of meditative and contemplative techniques available—or you might just want to sit quietly and relax.

Whenever you meditate, contemplate or "just sits," it's good to ask the white light to surround, fill and protect you, knowing only that which is for your highest good and the highest good of all concerned will take place during your meditation.

Before starting, prepare your physical environment. Arrange not to be disturbed. Unplug the phone. Put a note on the door. Wear ear plugs if noises might distract you. (We like the soft foam-rubber kind sold under such trade names as E.A.R., HUSHER and DECIDAMP.) Take care of your bodily needs. Have some water nearby if you get thirsty, and maybe some tissues, too.

Contemplation is thinking *about* something, often something of an uplifting nature. You could contemplate any of the hundreds of quotes or ideas in this book. Often, when we hear a new and potentially useful idea, we say, "I'll have to think about that." Contemplation is a good time to "think about that," to consider the truth of it, to imagine the changes and improvements it might make in your life.

Or, you could contemplate a nonverbal object, such as a flower, or a concept, such as God. The idea of contemplation is to set aside a certain amount of quiet time to think about just *that,* whatever you decide "that" will be.

Meditation. There are so many techniques of meditation, taught by so many organizations, that it's hard to define the word properly. We'll give a capsule summary of some techniques from John-Roger's book, *Inner Worlds of Meditation*. (For more complete descriptions, you can get the book for $7 postpaid, from Mandeville Press, Box 3935, Los Angeles, CA 90051.)

How beautiful it is
to do nothing,
and then rest afterward.

SPANISH PROVERB

You might want to try various meditations to see what they're like. With meditation, please keep in mind that *you'll never know until you do it*. We may somehow like to think we know what the effects of a given meditation will be just by reading the description, and that, in fact, is exactly what happens. We *think* we know; we don't *really* know. We suggest you try it, gain the experience, and decide from that more stable base of knowledge what is best for you at this time. And please remember to "call in the light" before beginning. We suggest you do not do these meditations while driving a car, operating dangerous machinery or where you need to be alert.

Breathing Meditation. Sit comfortably, close your eyes, and simply be aware of your breath. Follow it in and out. Don't "try" to breathe; don't consciously alter your rhythm of breathing; just follow the breath as it naturally flows in and out. If you get lost in thoughts, return to your breath. This can be a very refreshing meditation— twenty minutes can feel like a night's sleep. It's also especially effective when you're feeling emotionally upset.

Tones. Some people like to add a word or sound to help the mind focus as the breath goes in and out. Some people use *"one"* or God or AUM (OHM) or love. These— or any others—are fine. As you breathe in, say to yourself, mentally, "love." As you breathe out, "love." A few other tones you might want to try:

- **HU.** HU is an ancient sound for the higher power. One of the first names humans ever gave to a supreme being was HU. Some good words begin with HU: *humor, human, hub* (the center), *hug, huge, hue, humus* ("The Good Earth"), *humble,* and, of course, *hula.* HU is pronounced "Hugh." You can say it silently as you breathe in, and again as you breathe out. Or, you can pronounce the letter H on the inhale and the letter U on the exhale. You might also try saying HU out loud as you exhale, but don't do it out loud more than fifteen times in one sitting; the energies it produces can be powerful.

*True silence is
the rest of the mind;
it is to the spirit
what sleep is to the body,
nourishment and refreshment.*

WILLIAM PENN

- **ANI-HU.** This tone brings with it compassion, empathy and unity. You can chant it silently (ANI on the inhale, HU on the exhale) or out loud (ANI-HU on the exhale). It makes a lovely group chant and tends to harmonize the group—in more ways than one.

- **HOO.** This can be used like the HU. Some people prefer it. It's one syllable, pronounced like the word *who*.

- **RA.** RA is a tone for bringing great amounts of physical energy into the body. You can do it standing or sitting. Standing tends to bring in more energy. Take a deep breath and, as you exhale, chant, out loud, "ERRRRRRRAAAAAAAAA" until your air runs out. Take another deep breath and repeat it; then again. After three RAs, breathe normally for a few seconds. Then do another set of three, pause, then another set of three. We suggest you don't do more than three sets of three at any one time.

- **SO-HAWNG.** The SO-HAWNG meditation is a good one to use when your mind wants to do one thing and your emotions another. SO-HAWNG tends to unify the two, getting them on the same track. This tone is done silently. You breathe in on SO and out on HAWNG. Try it with your eyes closed for about five minutes and see how you feel. You may feel ready to accomplish some task you've been putting off for a long time.

- **THO.** THO is a tone of healing. The correct pronunciation of it is important. Take a deep breath, and as you breathe out say, "THooooo." The TH is accented; it's a sharp, percussive sound (and it may tickle your upper lip). It's followed by "ooooooo" as an extended version of the word *oh*. To do the THO meditation, sit comfortably, close your eyes, inhale and exhale twice, take a third deep breath, and on the third exhale, say, "THoooooo." Repeat three times this series of three breaths with THO aloud on the third breath. That's enough. It's powerful. Feel the

*Silence is the element
in which great things
fashion themselves together.*

THOMAS CARLYLE

healing energies move through your body. You can also chant THO inwardly as a formal meditation or any time during the day, even while doing something else. (But, again, as with all meditations, not while driving a car or operating potentially dangerous equipment.)

Flame Meditation. This uses the power of fire to dissolve negativity. Put a candle on a table and sit so you can look directly into the flame, not down on it. Allow your energy to flow *up* and *out* into the candle. You may feel negativity or have negative thoughts. Don't pay any attention to their content; just release them into the flame. If you feel your energy dropping back down inside of you as though you were going into a trance, blow out the candle and stop the meditation. The idea is to keep the energy flowing up and out and into the flame. Do it for no more than five minutes to start. See how you feel for a day or so afterward. You may have more vivid dreams. If you feel fine otherwise, you might try it for longer periods. Twenty minutes a day would be a lot.

Water Meditation. Take some water in a clear glass, hold it between your hands (without your hands touching each other), and simply look down into the glass. Observe whatever you observe. You may see colors. You may see energy emanating from your hands. You may just see yourself holding a glass of water. Observe the water for five minutes, gradually working up to fifteen. Drink the water at the end of the meditation. Your energies have made it a "tonic," giving you whatever you may need at that time. As an experiment, you can take two glasses, each half-filled with tap water. Set one aside, and do the water meditation with the other. Then taste each. Don't be surprised if the one you "charged" tastes different.

E. The E sound is chanted out loud after meditation to "ground" you and bring your focus back to the physical. It's a steady "Eeeeeeeeeeeee" as though you were pronouncing the letter E. It begins at the lower register of your voice, travels to the upper range, then back down again in one breath. You begin as a bass, go through

*I can't do no literary work for
the rest of this year because
I'm meditating another
lawsuit and looking around
for a defendant.*

MARK TWAIN

tenor, alto, onto soprano, and back to bass again. As you do this, imagine that the sound is in your feet when you're in the lower register, gradually going higher in your body as your voice goes higher, finally reaching the top of your head at the highest note of the eeee, and then back down your body as the voice lowers. If you try it, you'll see that it's far easier to do than it is to explain. Do two or three E sounds after each meditation session.

☆

These tones and meditations have worked for many people. We don't ask you to *believe* they work. We simply ask you, if you like, to try them and see what happens. If they do work, you don't need belief; you've got knowledge. Your results will dictate whether you'll use them often, sometimes, seldom or never. Some may work better for you than others; that's only natural. Use the ones that work best for you now and, every so often, return to the others to see if they will offer more.

Some people think meditation takes time *away* from physical accomplishment. Taken to extremes, of course, that's true. Most people, however, find that meditation *creates* more time than it *takes*.

Meditation is for rest, healing, balance and information. All these are helpful in the attainment of a goal. Here's an additional technique you might want to add to your meditation. It's designed to make both the meditation and the time outside of meditation more effective.

One of the primary complaints people have about meditating is, "My thoughts won't leave me alone." Perhaps the mind is trying to communicate something valuable. If the thought is something to do, write it down (or record it on a tape recorder). Then return to the meditation. This allows the mind to move onto something else—such as meditation, for example.

As the "to do" list fills, the mind empties. If the thought, "Call the bank," reappears, you need only tell the

Not merely an absence of noise,
Real Silence begins when
a reasonable being
withdraws from the noise
in order to find peace and
order in his inner sanctuary.
The exodus from slavery
toward the possession
of the Kingdom.

PETER MINARD

mind, "It's on the list. You can let that one go." And it will. (It is important, however, to *do* the things on the list—or at least to consider them from a nonmeditative state. If you don't, the mind will not pay any more attention to your writing it down than you do, and it will continue to bring it up, over and over.)

When finished meditating, not only will you have had a better meditation, you will also have a "to do" list that is very useful. One insight gleaned during meditation might save *hours,* perhaps *days* of unnecessary work. That's what we mean when we say—from a purely practical point of view—meditation can make more time than it takes.

*Money will come to you when
you are doing the right thing.*

MICHAEL PHILIPS

Seeding and Tithing

Seeding and tithing are two important aspects of achievement. One is saying "please," the other is saying "thank you."

Seeding and tithing are acknowledging the *source* of our good, our abundance. The source is whatever we choose that source to be—whichever organization represents the highest good you know. The acknowledgement is in the form of *money*.

Money, yes, money. By giving away *money,* it shows we *really mean it.* Just *whom* does it show we really mean it? Why, *ourselves,* of course. And it shows the comfort zone, too. There's little the comfort zone has a tighter hold on than the purse strings. If you can give away *money*—in set amounts and at regular intervals—your mastery of the comfort zone is well under way.

Seeding is giving money away *before* you get something. As its name implies, it is *planting a seed.* What would it be worth to you—in terms of hard cash—for you to have your Dream? Seed from one to ten percent of that amount. How do you seed? Send a check to the organization that represents—in your estimation—the highest power for good, and let it go.

Don't tell *anyone* that you have seeded for something until *after* you have obtained it. With your Dream, it's OK to tell certain friends the *Dream*—but keep your *seeding,* like your purpose, entirely to yourself.

Tithing is giving away ten percent of your material increase. If you make $1,000, give $100 of it away. If someone gives you something worth $1,000, give $100 (in cash or valuable asset) away.

Why? By tithing, you make a statement of abundance to yourself. You are saying, "Thank you. I have more than I need." To consistently give away ten percent of your increase indicates—through action—that you are a conscientious user of energy. Those who waste energy, it seems,

*No one would remember the
Good Samaritan if he only
had good intentions.
He had money as well.*

MARGARET THATCHER

are given less and less. Those who make good use of it are given more and more. Tithing demonstrates you are a good manager of resources.

Where you give your money is not important. If you have no spiritual or religious affiliation (the traditional depository of seeding and tithing), you can give to your favorite charity or social cause. Just so it represents to you the *highest* and *best* work being done on the planet, any organization—or person—is fine.

In terms of seeding and tithing, you could just as well throw the money out the window. *Where* it goes is not as important as *that* it goes. It's the spirit with which you part with it that counts.

One more thought: if you give begrudgingly, it will be given unto you begrudgingly. If you give joyfully, it will be given unto you joyfully.

Don't wait to give, however, until you can do it joyfully. It's a mechanical process. Being given to begrudgingly is better than not being given to at all.

(More information on seeding and tithing is in John-Roger's book *Wealth and Higher Consciousness* which is available for $12.00 from Mandeville Press, Box 3935, Los Angeles, CA 90051. 213-737-4055).

Be bold—
and mighty forces will
come to your aid.

BASIL KING

The Willingness to Do
Creates the Ability to Do

When looking at all that must be done to fulfill our Dream, it's easy to wonder, "How am I going to *do* all this?" Don't worry about *how* you'll do the work, just be *willing* to do the work.

Be *willing* to get off your butt.

You can start by using your (other) *buts* to your benefit. When the comfort zone creates a limiting thought, you can add, "...but I'm willing to _____." "I don't know how to do this...but I'm willing to know." "I'm too tired to do this...but I'm willing to have the energy." "I'm not worthy of this...but I'm willing to be worthy."

The willingness opens the doors to knowledge, direction and achievement. Be willing to know, be willing to do, be willing to create a positive result.

Be willing, especially, to follow your Dream.

If you have built castles in the air,
your work need not be lost;
that is where they should be.
Now put the foundations under them.

HENRY DAVID THOREAU

Just Do It!

ADVERTISEMENT FOR RUNNING SHOES

PART FIVE

DOING IT

We're going to be moving even faster. (We can just *feel* that Divine Patience *barely* keeping Divine Impatience in check.)

The mind and the emotions (your passion) are now in alignment behind your Dream (or moving in that direction more and more each moment). Now it's time for *action*— to *DO IT!*

Laziness is nothing more than the habit of resting before you get tired.

JULES RENARD

The Biggest Lie in Action

The biggest lie we tell ourselves in the area of action is, "I'll do it later." As C. Northcote Parkinson expressed it, "Delay is the deadliest form of denial."

Putting things off is known, of course, as procrastination. We know that "pro" means *for,* but we don't know what "crastination" means. Maybe it means *laziness.* Maybe it means *don't go after your Dream, but kid yourself into thinking that someday you will.* Whatever crastination means, we're against it.

You could say we're pro anticrastination.

(Actually, we *do* know what crastination means— *crastinus* is Latin for things pertaining to *tomorrow.* *Pro*crastinus is "putting things off till tomorrow," "Never put off till tomorrow," Mark Twain said, "what you can do the day after tomorrow." *Procrastinus-crastinus?)*

The interesting thing about "later" is that it can never be proven false. One can never reproach us. If confronted, we can always say, "I said I'd do it later. It's not later yet."

In this way, we can put off and put off and put off *indefinitely.* We only run out of laters when we run out of breath. Death is nature's way of saying, "No more laters left." By then, of course, who cares?

It's not "who cares?" when you're dead that counts, it's "who cares?" while you're still alive. The answer to that question is *you.* Somehow we know how many laters we have stockpiled from the past. We know that adding another later to that pile is like adding a grain of sand to a beach. Somehow, we know we're probably never going to get back to that particular grain of sand.

We know that "later" is a lie.

If you can do something now, do it now. If it can't be done now, decide (A) it's not going to get done, or (B) *when* it will get done.

If you trap the moment before it's ripe,
The tears of repentance
    you'll certainly wipe;
But if once you let the ripe moment go
You can never wipe off the tears of woe.

WILLIAM BLAKE
1791

He who hesitates is poor.

ZERO MOSTEL
THE PRODUCERS

If something doesn't get done, and you decide you will still do it, schedule a *specific date and time* when it will get done. *Schedule* the activity in. Write it in your appointment book. If it's not worth the amount of time it takes to schedule it *now,* it's probably not going to get done "later."

As the guru once said to procrastinating disciples, "You're in your laters now." All those things we put off until "later" return—to be put off until "later" again, and again.

Do them, or declare them done.

When we put things off until some future—probably mythical—Laterland, we drag the past into the future. The burden of yesterday's incompletions is a heavy load to carry. *Don't carry it.*

A Dream is an ephemeral thing. To travel to it, you have to travel light. "I travel light;" Christopher Fry wrote, "as light, that is, as a man can travel who will still carry his body around because of its sentimental value."

Getting in the habit of doing what needs to be done as it presents itself to be done—whether it *needs* to be done in that moment or not—creates an inner freedom for the next moment, the next activity.

Such as, oh, pursuing your Dream.

*Have no fear
of perfection—
you'll never reach it.*

SALVADOR DALI

We're Not Perfect—We're Human

How do we learn? By doing—*including* those things we have to learn how to do before we can do them. As Aristotle said: "For the things we have to learn before we can do them, we learn by doing them." Yes, *everything* is best learned by doing.

A primary reason people don't do new things is because they want to be able to do them perfectly—first time. It's completely irrational, impractical, not workable—and yet, it's how most people run their lives. It's called The Perfection Syndrome.

Whoever said we had to do it perfect?

Our parents. And if not our parents, there were those bastions of perfection—school teachers. (The ones who would point out that the last paragraph should read, "Whoever said we had to do it perfect*ly?*" They would also point out that paragraphs should be more than one sentence long.)

For the most part, we weren't taught to set goals and to achieve them. In addition, we had to achieve a goal in "the right way." Perfection was not just "do it right," but also "do it *my way.*" Merely *reaching* the goal was not good enough. The goal had to be attained the way someone else (whoever was teaching us) thought was the "best way" (that is, *their* way).

We say, don't worry—just DO IT!

Don't worry about "right way"; don't worry about "my way." DO IT! When it's all said and done—when you've reached your goal—you can look back and discover what *your* way really was. As Margaret Mead said, "The best way to do field work is not to come up for air until you're done." Amen.

Most people have an image of themselves that's "perfect." If they can't perform according to their own imaginary standards of perfection, they "take their ball and go home." As Cardinal Newman observed, "Nothing would

When in doubt,
make a fool of yourself.
There is a microscopically thin
line between being brilliantly
creative and acting like the
most gigantic idiot on earth.
So what the hell, leap.

CYNTHIA HEIMEL

be done at all if a man waited until he could do it so well that no one could find fault with it."

"Men would like to learn to love themselves, but they usually find they cannot," Gerald Brenan explained. "That is because they have built an ideal image of themselves which puts their real self in the shade."

This "ideal image" of ourselves—the one that's "perfect" and won't let anyone see us as other than perfect—we must send on a long field trip somewhere. Maybe Alpha Centauri.

The only way to even *approach* doing something perfectly is through experience, and experience, as Oscar Wilde observed, "is the name everyone gives to their mistakes."

Mistakes are excellent teachers. Sir Humphrey Davy wrote, "I have learned more from my mistakes than from my successes." Make as many mistakes as you can, as quickly as you can. "Show me a guy who's afraid to look bad," said Rene Auberjonis, "and I'll show you a guy you can beat every time." Set out each day to look foolish, stupid, blundering, awkward—anything you consider the perfect representation of *im*perfect.

In this way, you shatter the false image of a "perfect self," and get used to being a stumble-through-it, catch-as-catch-can, make-do, seat-of-the-pants, mistake-making human being—just like every other successful dreamer.

After all, it's not perfect being perfect.

*The superior man thinks
always of virtue;
the common man thinks
of comfort.*

CONFUCIUS

Be Prepared to Be Scared

When we put ourselves on the path of expansion by committing to a goal that's outside our comfort zone, one thing's for certain—we're going to be given a lot of opportunities to expand. One additional thing is certain—we are *not* going to be able to choose all those opportunities for expansion.

Our choice is either "expand" or "contract." If we choose "expand," we will expand—and we'll *always* wish there were more comfortable ways of doing it.

Let's say someone's goal was to get her body in shape. The *way* this would happen, she imagines, is in a sparkling health club with chrome-plated barbells and Tom Cruise holding her feet while she does situps. How, she wonders, will the money "materialize" so that she can pay for the queen's ransom of a membership?

Meanwhile, in the first week after committing to her goal, her car runs out of gas, and she has to walk five miles to the nearest phone; an emergency happens at work and she is asked to fill in, packing boxes in the warehouse; her freezer was accidently unplugged and all her ice cream melted; and, on the weekend, she goes on a spiritual retreat, hoping to get some rest. All weekend, however, was devoted to what they called "dharma yoga," which sounded nice *in principle,* but in reality was digging ditches, cutting down trees and helping a pair of not-so-busy beavers build a dam.

At the end of the first week, she had lost five pounds, taken an inch off her waist, and looked better—but felt sorer—than she had in years.

This is how it happens. We get the Dream, but we don't get to dictate every step toward the Dream.

We can, of course, refuse to do the uncomfortable activity placed in front of us. When we know something *might* move us a step closer to our goal, and we choose

*Minds, like bodies,
will often fall into a pimpled,
ill-conditioned state from mere
excess of comfort.*

CHARLES DICKENS

not to do it "because it's uncomfortable," we are also choosing not to pursue our goal. It's that simple.

This refusal has two results. First, we are not that one step closer to our goal. Second, the opportunities to expand—to reach the goal—will, in the future, be less significant, and presented less frequently.

When we *un*commit through inaction (honoring the comfort zone), the success fulfillment mechanism backs off, too. Our success fulfillment mechanism is not there to *hurt* us, it's there to *help* us. If we indicate—through nonaction—that we aren't ready to take the steps necessary to reach the goal, it says, "Fine. Let me know when you're ready."

It's as though we went to a friend's house for the evening. After asking three or four times in the first hour if we wanted anything to drink, and our response was always, "No, thank you," our host would, naturally, ask less frequently, and, eventually, stop.

Whatever you find *most* uncomfortable, be willing to do it. You may not *have* to do it, but be *willing* to. Your willingness will be tested. If you say, "I'm willing!" and the opportunity arises and you're *not,* then, evidently, you're not.

When a given portion of the comfort zone is being expanded, it always *seems* as though expansion of *any other part* would be more tolerable, more acceptable. We want to put it off, postpone, and do it later, when some *other* part of the comfort zone can be challenged.

In fact, when that *other* part is challenged, it will seem as though *this* is the worst part of the comfort zone, and *any other* area would be better than *this.* Discomfort always seems more tolerable anywhere other than the place in which it's being felt.

The solution? *Plan* to be uncomfortable. Understand that it's a necessary part of the process for success. Learn to be comfortable with discomfort. Have compassion for the part of you that's growing. The first step is a *willingness* to be uncomfortable.

*One of the best ways to properly
evaluate and adapt to the many
environmental stresses of life is to
simply view them as normal.
The adversity and failures in our
lives, if adapted to and viewed as
normal corrective feedback to use
to get back on target,
serve to develop in us an immunity
against anxiety, depression, and the
adverse responses to stress.
Instead of tackling the most important
priorities that would make us
successful and effective in life,
we prefer the path of least resistance
and do things simply that will
relieve our tension,
such as shuffling papers and
majoring in minors.*

DENIS WAITLEY

The next step is to realize *which* emotion from the comfort zone you're feeling each time you feel "uncomfortable." Fear? Guilt? Unworthiness? Hurt feelings? Anger? Observe it. See if you can locate it in the body.

As we mentioned earlier, fear is probably the most frequently felt of the comfort zone's emotions. Not only do we feel fear, but also fear every other comfort-zone emotion. Unworthiness, for example, seldom has to make an appearance. The *fear* of unworthiness is enough to keep most people in check. If you feel fear, ask yourself if the fear is being afraid of *something,* or it's being afraid of feeling another *emotion.*

The final step is turning your *perception* of each "negative" emotion into its positive counterpart. Learn to see fear as excitement, guilt as the energy for personal change, unworthiness as the discipline to live your Dream, hurt feelings as caring, and anger as the energy for outer change.

This reprogramming can take some time. Do not, however, wait until you have the "conversion technique" mastered before moving—steadily and persistently—toward your Dream. Some people are past their first Dream and well on the way to their second before they can even locate the comfort zone's feelings in the body.

For now, be willing to be uncomfortable. Be comfortable being uncomfortable. It may get tough, but it's a small price to pay for living your Dream.

Guilt is never a rational thing;
it distorts all the faculties of
the human mind,
it perverts them,
it leaves a man no longer in
the free use of his reason,
it puts him into confusion.

EDMUND BURKE

Guilt (again)

We're going to briefly discuss guilt—*again*. It's probably the most insidious citizen of the comfort zone.

Fear increases as we come closer and closer to actually *doing* the thing we're afraid to do. Let's say we're afraid of walking up to a stranger in a supermarket and saying, "Hello." We have decided that meeting strangers is a necessary part of reaching our Dream (a Marriage/Family dream, for example). So, the next "perfect stranger" we see in a public place—we are *committed* to walk up and say, "Hello, I'd like to meet you."

There's the stranger and here we are, with nothing between us but the canned peas. Emotion: fear. No, it's *not* excitement—no matter how many times we've read that chapter, *Fear is the Energy to Do Your Best in a New Situation*. This is a new situation, and this is *fear—panic*.

We know, however, that we must do this thing. We have gone over it and over it in our mind and with supportive friends. This may or may not be *our* perfect stranger, but this *is* the perfect opportunity to "move through fear," to "feel the fear and do it anyway."

No matter *what* happens, at least we will have learned to meet new people, so that some enchanted evening, if we see a stranger across a crowded room, we can fly to their side and make them our own, so that all through our life we won't have to dream all alone.

We take one step in the direction of the stranger. The stranger's head moves—maybe to *look* at us! We grab a can of peas and begin studying the label intensely.

This is *silly*, we tell ourselves. We are an *adult*. We are *committed*. The blood courses in our ears. Our heart is pounding. We take charge of the situation, and we *act*.

"Do you think these peas are as good as the ones on sale?" we ask the stranger.

*Guilt is the source of sorrows,
the avenging fiend that
follows us behind
with whips and stings.*

NICHOLAS ROWE

"Gee, I don't know," the stranger replies. "I only buy fresh peas myself." We notice the stranger is wearing a wedding ring. Hummm. *Not* the perfect stranger after all.

"Oh, of course," we smile. "Thank you."

That's a fairly typical move-through-fear situation. Before it, we can pep-talk ourselves, and we can rah-rah our way through it. We can physically *feel* the comfort zone becoming more and more dense as we begin doing the thing we're afraid to do. That's all fear.

Guilt is all the rest we live with after.

Guilt picks its own moments—not *moment*, but *moments,* lots of them. Two minutes later. An hour later. A week later, at three in the morning, when we wake up in a cold sweat. Two weeks later, when we can't get to sleep.

We are berated for moving through the fear. We are reminded of a story on the news about someone meeting another a person in a supermarket and the terrible things that happened to them *that could have happened to us*. Guilt projects an endless succession of "What-ifs" across our inner nightmare gallery.

If we don't give in to the chatterings that we *shouldn't* have done it in the first place—if we hold firmly to the idea that walking up to strangers and meeting them is part of our Dream, and that we're going to continue doing it no matter *what* guilt says—then the guilt changes its tack.

"Why didn't you see that the stranger was wearing a wedding ring?" guilt asks. "Why aren't you more observant? You went through all that for *nothing*. Besides, your commitment was to say, 'Hello, I'd like to meet you,' not to discuss canned vegetables. You can't even do *that* right."

And on and on.

If the guilt gets us on any of these, and we agree to be more, well, *something* next time—something less than what we know we could be—guilt floods us with positive feelings. We feel a sense of freedom and joy that must parallel enlightenment. Euphoric feelings rush in.

*If you're going
to do something wrong,
at least enjoy it.*

LEO ROSTEN

"Of course," we say, "this restriction is *me*. I *choose* to have it. It's part of *who I am*." With each statement of limitation, we soar higher and higher.

Guilt cannot only make us feel terrible, it can also make us feel wonderful.

Guilt is a trainer with both sugar cubes and a cattle prod. When we tow the mark—the confines of the comfort zone—we get sweetness. When we "overstep our bounds," we get punished.

The next time we *don't* walk up to a stranger, we are rewarded with a good feeling and a pep talk. This is the booby prize of life.

So, how to use guilt *for* ourselves? As the old Hindu saying says, "It takes a thorn to remove a thorn," or, as we say in the West, "Fight fire with fire." Start feeling guilty when you *don't* take steps toward your Dream. Feel all those guilt-things when you *honor* the comfort zone.

Yes, for a while, this will put you in any number of dammed-if-I-do-and-dammed-if-I-don't situations—you're going to feel guilty no matter *how* you act. Eventually, however, guilt will be the staunch ally to your Dream that it is currently to your comfort zone.

This is also a place where *external support* comes in handy—a friend, counselor, therapist or support group—to encourage you to continue taking risks, to continue moving toward your Dream.

*My philosophy is that
not only are you responsible
for your life,
but doing the best
at this moment
puts you in the best place
for the next moment.*

OPRAH WINFREY

Response Ability

Responsibility is a misunderstood word. Most people use it to mean blame. "Who's responsible for this?" means "Who's to blame for this? Whom can I punish?"

We are experts at finding blame. We blame others for not making us happy, for letting us down, for not fulfilling our dreams. If people become involved in personal growth or therapy of some kind, they frequently don't become more responsible—they just find new things to blame. Childhood! Parents! Heredity! Environment!

Let's blame our parents for programming us to blame others, shall we?

Enough! It's time to grow up. If we want to play adult games—living our Dream—we must play by adult rules. One of the primary adult rules: We are individually responsible for our own lives.

Responsible simply means, "The ability to respond." In any of life's challenges, opportunities or disasters, we can *respond* in whatever way we choose. Our response dictates what life hands us next. Our response was either a workable response (it took us one step closer to our goal) or an unworkable response (it did *not* take us one step closer to our goal).

It's not a matter of right/wrong, good/bad. It's a matter of *practical analysis* of the situation. From *that* situation, we have the ability to respond again. When the outcome of that is known, we will either be closer to, or farther from, our goal. Then we have the ability to respond to *that*.

And so it goes. The one common denominator in our lives, as adults, is *us*. In everything we experience, there is *one person* who is *always there*. It's not mommy and it's not daddy—it's *us*.

In addition to what we can do *physically* about a situation, we also have the ability to choose what our *inner* response to that situation is.

If you are distressed by anything
external, the pain is not due to the
thing itself, but to your estimate of it;
and this you have the power to revoke
at any moment.

MARCUS AURELIUS
(121-180)

The greatest discovery of my generation
is that a human being can alter his life by
altering his attitudes of mind.

WILLIAM JAMES
(1842-1910)

This is a big one. It sounds like a radical new idea, but it's not. It's centuries old. The idea is this: what happens in the outer environment has *nothing to do* with how we *respond* to what happens in the outer environment.

Dr. Albert Ellis has been a major proponent of this theory in our time. The title *alone* of one of his books activates comfort zones: *How to Stubbornly Refuse to Make Yourself Miserable About Anything—Yes, Anything!*

In reading that title, most people begin to list all those things they are *entitled* to feel *miserable* about. These are usually catastrophic losses, and, yes, we do feel bad about those. For significant losses, there is a mourning process we must go through. (If you're faced with this situation, please read a book by Melba Colgrove, Ph.D., Harold H. Bloomfield, M.D., and Peter McWilliams entitled *How to Survive the Loss of a Love.* 1-800-LIFE-101.) We're not talking here about significant losses.

We're talking about the daily slings-and-arrows for which we feel quite justified in blaming someone or something outside ourselves. Yes, it was the milkman's *fault* the milk wasn't delivered, but our negative inner *reaction* to that situation is all ours.

Are we going to cry over undelivered milk? If we really want the milk, we're going to have to make alternate arrangements, and those arrangements are going to have to be made *regardless* of how miserable we make ourselves.

This is a big concept. It challenges us in a fundamental way. To reeducate ourselves is not easy. Our culture *supports* and *encourages* our deeply rooted programming that what happens "out there" is directly connected to what happens "in here." (See? We just blamed the *culture* for making it *difficult.)*

Please remember: it is OK to feel good when things go bad. Being content, satisfied and joyful no matter *what* happens is a radical concept—but it's also basic rule of adult life.

Without this rule—to at least *aspire* to—we live in a land of Victims and Victors, of endless finger-pointing and

BLANCHE: *I'm reading this Spock
book on baby care,
and he says it's very important
for a young child to have
a male role model around
during its formative years.
Now what are we gonna do?...*

ROSE: *Oh, Blanche, we don't have
anything to worry about.
If we give that baby love and
attention and understanding,
it'll turn out fine.*

DOROTHY: *That's beautiful.*

ROSE: *Besides, what does Spock
know about raising babies?
On Vulcan, all the kids
are born in pods.*

THE GOLDEN GIRLS

name-calling. Even if we *can* affix blame, so what? If we need to get the milk, *we need to get the milk*. If you want to fulfill your Dream, look more for "What's next?" than "Who's wrong?"

Our inner life reflects our outer, and our outer life reflects our inner. We suggest making changes in *both*. When a situation arises, ask yourself, "What response can I make—inner, outer, or both—that would get me closer to my goal?" These are more useful questions than, "Whom can I punish?" (Most often, the answer to, "Whom can I punish?" is *us*. It's guilt's favorite question.)

Start by forgiving your parents. They didn't have a manual on raising kids—not a complete one, anyway. Besides, *they* didn't raise us, *we* raised us. We chose from all that happened to us to sink or swim, rise or fall. Many great people—however you'd like to define the word "great"—had more miserable childhoods than we did, and somehow they managed to be great.

We have the same opportunities for greatness. They happen every day, every minute. Do we learn a lesson, or blame the teacher? The teacher could be a flat tire, a broken agreement, or undelivered milk. Do we look into the mirror and change ourselves, or do we break it? Do we pursue our Dream, or have all the reasonable reasons why not?

Next week there can't be any crisis.
My schedule is already full.

HENRY A. KISSINGER

Most modern calendars mar the sweet
simplicity of our lives by reminding us
that each day that passes is the
anniversary of some perfectly
uninteresting event.

OSCAR WILDE

We Don't Plan to Fail,
We Just Fail to Plan

It's a well-known fact: long-range planning never works. We almost always get to our goal through means *other* than the ones we put on our schedule. So why plan? Because people who *don't* make long-range plans seldom get to where they want to be.

In short, a plan will get you to your goal, but not in the way that's on the plan.

So, plan. And, be prepared not just to change *horses* in midstream, but to change to a *boat* in midstream. Keep your goal, your Dream. Stay firm and fixed on that. Be prepared, however, for whatever methods come along to get you there. *Especially* methods not on your plan. Plan on it.

How to plan? Simple. Take a segment of time, take a goal, and divide up the latter into the former. Keep dividing it up until you have a *next action step*—something you can do *right now* to move toward your goal.

Let's say you want to produce a play within the next year. Get some kind of calendar that divides a year into units with which we're all familiar—months, weeks, days, etc. Twelve months from now, write, "Play opens." You have the goal (the play), and you have the time (twelve months). Now, chop up the goal.

What needs to happen before the play opens? Make a list. One item per 3x5 card is good, or list them on a sheet of paper. This list doesn't need to be in any particular order. Brainstorm. Free-associate.

When the list is complete, put it in order, according to time. What needs to happen first, second, and so forth. "Find a play," for example, would probably come before, "Design the posters."

If something is a toss-up ("Do I find the play or the director first?"), choose the way in which you would *like* it

*The journey of ten thousand
miles begins with
a single phone call.*

CONFUCIUS BELL

to go, and schedule that. Remember: little of this will go this way, but if you don't do it, you won't get a play. (If Shakespeare can end a scene with a couplet, we can end a paragraph with one.)

Now, start laying these out *backwards* in time. How many weeks of rehearsal? Six weeks? Put those in. That means casting and theater will have to be completed by six weeks before a year from now. How much time do you want to work with the director before casting? Put that time in. Continue.

When everything is roughly laid out, you can ask yourself, "Is a year enough time? Is a year too much time?" Let's say a year is a good period of time—not too ambitious, not too lethargic.

Continue breaking the plan down until you know what you must do *next*—something specific you can actually, physically *do*. "Find a play," is too vague. "Call these twelve people and let them know I'm looking for a play," is a workable next action step. This might be followed by, "Read plays submitted." That's a do-able action step.

When the plays *are* submitted, the action steps become more precise, "Read *DO IT! The Musical!*" would be a next do-able action step. (And an excellent one, too, we might add. It has this great opening number, called *Let's Get Off Our Buts,* and there's this marvelous scene with the dancing comfort zone—like the plant in *Little Shop of Horrors*—and, well, a word to the wise producer is sufficient.)

Now, start *scheduling* the next action steps. *When* will you call the twelve people on the list? "Next week" is not good enough for that one. *When* next week? What *day?* What *time?* Schedule it in. If you don't have an appointment book or calendar of some kind, by all means get one.

Don't wait until you have the "perfect" one. ("I plan to research time-scheduling systems real soon now.") If you don't have one, *any* one is better than what you have. (And when you want a great one—and a productivity course to go with it—call ICG at 213-829-2100.)

Writing is easy.
All you do is stare at a blank sheet of
paper until drops of blood
form on your forehead.

GENE FOWLER

The writer's only responsibility
is to his art.
He will be completely ruthless
if he is a good one. He has a dream.
Everything goes by the board:
honor, pride, decency, security, happiness, all,
to get the book written.
If a writer has to rob his mother,
he will not hesitate;
the "Ode on a Grecian Urn"
is worth any number of old ladies.

WILLIAM FAULKNER

When you diagram your Big Dream, plan to do *something* on it every day. Remember when we suggested that if you don't plan to devote at least fourteen hours per week—two hours per day—to your Dream, maybe it's not a big enough Dream, or maybe you don't really want it? Here's where that Dream begins to manifest—in the fourteen (or more) hours per week you schedule it into your calendar. The fourteen hours *next week* you schedule it into your calendar. The two (or more) hours you schedule it in *tomorrow,* and the next day, and the day after that.

They can be general things—completing this book, for example, or making some exploratory phone calls, or, if you *are* a producer, finding out if there really *is* a musical version of *DO IT!* Your Dream may have some very specific action steps that can be scheduled today—or tomorrow, at the latest. "I will write from 6:00 to 8:00 a.m. tomorrow."

What does writing look like? Seat-of-the-pants-in-the-seat-of-the-chair. The output may be one word or one thousand. For writing (meditating, phone calling, or any number of things), getting off our *buts* means getting *on* our *butts*—putting it into a chair and *not moving from the chair* for a set period of time.

Don't plan specific events too far in advance, especially early on in a project. One exploratory phone call might change the entire course of your project—a method may appear that's far better than any you may have considered yourself. Expect that. *Do* plan specific *amounts* of time doing *something* on your Dream *every day*. Those segments of time will fill as the project rolls (and flies) along.

Someone once said, "A blank sheet of paper is God's way of letting you know what it feels like to be God." So is a blank calendar. A calendar for the next year represents your *time,* one of the most precious commodities you have. Use it well. Choosing what you want to do, and when to do it, is an act of creation.

You are creating your Dream.

If you want to be a writer—
stop talking about it and sit down and write!

JACKIE COLLINS

The multitude of books is a great evil.
There is no limit to this fever for writing.

MARTIN LUTHER

It took me fifteen years to discover that I had
no talent for writing, but I couldn't give it up
because by then I was too famous.

ROBERT BENCHLEY

God is love, but get it in writing.

GYPSY ROSE LEE

Write Things Down

Everyone is a professional writer. You may not get paid for writing *per se* (the first rule of writing is never use the phrase *per se*—the New Yorker once had a cartoon of a street sign that read, "No parking, *per se*"), but you will be well-paid for what you write down.

Make lists of things—things to do, people to call, letters to write. In fulfilling your Dream, you're in business for yourself. Pursue your Dream with all the tools of the business world. One of the basic tools is listmaking.

People who want to appear clever rely on memory. People who want to get things done make lists. Even if you're good at remembering things, write them down anyway. That way, you don't have to remember them. Your mind is free for more creative pursuits.

The two enemies of memory are *time* and *volume*. Over time, we tend to forget. (Who sat two rows behind you in third grade?) And, when there's too much to remember, we forget. Write it all down.

Make notes of phone conversations. Most of these notes you'll never look at again, but when they come in handy, *they come in handy*.

Send letters to people confirming things, and cards thanking people for spending time with you on the phone. (You'll be getting lots of favors as you move toward your Dream.) These letters and cards can be handwritten— sometimes while you're still talking with the person. It's a nice gesture, and when you need another favor (and you will), the person is more likely to remember you fondly.

Dare we end this chapter by saying, "Write on!" No, we're professional writers. That's a cheap pun, and, although it may amuse a few people, it might make us look foolish.

Write on!

(We told *you* to take risks. Why shouldn't we take some, too? Which, in fact, segues neatly into the next chapter.)

*Every man has the right
to risk his own life
in order to save it.*

JEAN-JACQUES ROUSSEAU

Taking Risks

As often as we are counseled to "take risks" by the successful people of the world, that's about as often as that counsel is ignored. For the vast, vast majority of people, taking risks is just too, well, *risky*.

If we don't take risks, however, it's doubtful we'll ever get to our Dream. "A lot of successful people are risk-takers," Phillip Adams wrote, "Unless you're willing to do that, to have a go, to fail miserably, and have another go, success won't happen."

There must be *something* risky between you and your Dream, otherwise, why wouldn't you be living it? Attaining dreams requires new behavior, and new behavior is taking a risk.

"Be daring, be different, be impractical," Sir Cecil Beaton advised, "be anything that will assert integrity of purpose and imaginative vision against the play-it-safers, the creatures of the commonplace, the slaves of the ordinary."

"There are risks and costs to a program of action," John F. Kennedy said, "but they are far less than the long-range risks and costs of comfortable inaction."

Of course, there are limits. Andy Warhol had a suggestion for Kennedy and his kind: "The president has so much good publicity potential that hasn't been exploited. He should just sit down one day and make a list of all the things that people are embarrassed to do that they shouldn't be embarrassed to do, and then do them all on television."

A great idea from Mr. Warhol. Unfortunately, none of our presidents have taken him up on it—not *intentionally,* at any rate.

The irony is that the person *not* taking risks feels the same amount of fear as the person who *regularly* takes risks. The non-risk-taker simply feels the *same* amount of fear over more *trivial* things.

*Don't play for safety—
it's the most dangerous thing
in the world.*

HUGH WALPOLE

Understand that failure is part of the process. We told you about our publishing *successes,* but have we told you about our *failures?* To quote Jack Benny, "Well!" They were something.

People not taking calculated risks, designed to pursue their Dream, sometimes take foolish risks. They drive too fast, drink too much, abuse drugs, or engage in some other reckless behavior. "Take calculated risks," George Patton advised, "That is quite different from being rash."

Maybe the risk-taking mechanism in these rash individuals needs to be exercised—or maybe they want to prove (to themselves as much as to others) that they're not so cowardly after all. If they *really* wanted to display their courage, all they'd have to do is pursue their dreams.

The reverse of that is more often true. Having given up on their dreams, many give up on life, and die a little more each day. As Benjamin Franklin wrote, "Some people die at twenty-five and aren't buried until they are seventy-five." Or, to quote Auntie Mame's famous line, "Life is a banquet, and some poor sons-of-bitches are starving to death."

The thing you fear: all you have to do is walk right up and confront it. It's among the hardest things to do, but it's the only thing to be done. If you turn from it, it will bite you in the butt. The farther you run from it, the farther you run from your Dream. "Do the thing you fear," wrote Emerson, "and the death of fear is certain."

"Often the difference between a successful man and a failure is not one's better abilities or ideas," Maxwell Maltz observed, "but the courage that one has to bet on his ideas, to take a calculated risk—and to act."

*The greatest obstacle to
discovery is not ignorance—
it is the illusion of knowledge.*

DANIEL J. BOORSTIN

Don't Say No till You Know What You're Saying No to

As we mentioned before, when we commit to a goal, the methods to achieve that goal will appear. When the methods do appear, they may not be (and seldom are) dressed in familiar garb.

Many people are in the habit of saying "no" to all new experiences. Part of this, of course, is the comfort zone—"It's new, so don't do it."

Alas, saying no to something before we know what we're saying no to has a rather nasty name—one that no one likes to hear applied to themselves. That word is *prejudice*. It means, of course, to *pre-judge* something. Human beings do it all the time. How many opinions do you have of people you have never even met? Oh, you may not know them *personally,* but your opinions are accurate because you read about them in the *papers*. That's very different, then. (Uh-huh.)

We've had the chance to meet a number of famous people whom we initially "knew" only through the media. Many of them lived up to (or down to) their reputations. Others did not. Some people who had "bad reps" in the press were, in fact, delightful. (As Hedda Hopper said, "Nobody's interested in sweetness and light.") Others, who are known to be magnificent individuals, were, in fact, monsters.

Many people say no because they don't want to know. "The mind of a bigot is like the pupil of an eye;" wrote Oliver Wendell Holmes, Jr., "the more light you pour upon it, the more it will contract." We, of course, recommend becoming a pupil *of* light; a pupil of life.

"My mind is made up," the old saying goes, "don't try and confuse me with the facts." The answer to this comes from Aldous Huxley, "Facts do not cease to exist because they are ignored." William S. Burroughs gave the tendency to make up our minds before we have enough

*Try everything once
except incest and folk dancing.*

SIR THOMAS BEECHAM

information an even more severe interpretation: "A paranoid is a man who knows *a little* of what's going on."

If something presents itself to you, and you don't know enough about it to *really* decide if it might help you achieve your goal, don't say no—find out more. How do we find out more? By asking, doing, listening—in short, by getting involved; *experiencing*.

As you may have gathered by now, our advice on new opportunities is: if it's not going to *physically* harm you, and it *might* be helpful on the path to your Dream—try it. Other than the comfort zone's control of your life, what have you got to lose?

Another reason people don't even want to *hear* about new opportunities is that people are afraid to say no—especially after they've "gotten to know someone." It's the old don't-say-no-to-people-you-know-but-do-say-no-to-people-you-don't-know rule. It's a rule perpetrated by the people we know—for obvious reasons. ("Why are you giving your money to this charity to save *eagles* when *your own brother* needs new carpeting?")

This phenomenon was described by the great philosopher Gypsy Rose Lee: "She's descended from a long line her mother listened to." It's easier for most people to say no while the person offering the new experience is still a stranger.

No, we're not suggesting you listen to the spiel of *every* person who tries to sell you a flower at the airport. It is safe to assume that one besuited flower-seller will tell you about the same thing as any other. We are suggesting, however, that you listen to it *once*.

For things that are more clearly on your path, you might try them more than once. As Virgil Thomson—who thrived until his death at ninety-three—once said, "Try a thing you haven't done three times. Once, to get over the fear of doing it. Twice, to learn how to do it. And a third time to figure out whether you like it or not." The *other* famous Virgil (the one who lived 70-19 B.C.) seemed to agree, "Fortune sides with him who dares."

All men should try to learn
before they die
what they are running from,
and to, and why.

JAMES THURBER

Mr. Thomson has an excellent point. Doing something *once* will get us over the *fear* of doing it. That's fine, but, if it was a significant challenge to our comfort zone, it's not enough to feel *free* about it—there's still *guilt* to reckon with. Doing something *three times,* works through the fear of doing it, the fear of feeling guilty about doing it, and takes a good slice out of the guilt of doing it.

We are not free to *choose* to do a thing or not until it's fully *within* our comfort zone. "Freedom *from* something is not enough," observed Zechariah Chafee, Jr. "It should also be freedom *for* something."

The person who has never been to New York City—but has heard nasty things about it—is not free regarding New York City. The person who's been there *once,* and found some of the bad things people said were true, but discovered a lot of good things, too, is more free to choose to visit New York again. The person who's visited New York City often enough to feel comfortable there is completely free to choose to travel to New York or not.

After listening to people present whatever it is they have to present to you, then you can say no. You are not obligated to say yes just because you *listened*. You are only obligated if you *committed* to a certain course of action. Listening to information is not an agreement to do anything *with* the information. You may decide that the information is all very interesting, but it doesn't help you fulfill *your* dream. Say no, and be on your way. You may also find that you occasionally do something that is a complete waste of time. Oh, well. As someone once said, "Don't be afraid to go on an occasional wild goose chase. That's what wild geese are for." Or, to quote Flip Wilson, "You can't expect to hit the jackpot if you don't put a few nickels in the machine."

You may find, however, that the information *is* valuable. Remember that your goal-fulfillment system is working all the time—pulling experiences, lessons, information and people to you to help you fulfill your Dream. "Let your hook always be cast," Ovid said two thousand years ago. "In the pool where you least expect it, will be a fish."

*There is the greatest practical
benefit in making a few
failures early in life.*

T. H. HUXLEY

The Value of Action

There are two primary benefits to action.

The first is obvious, although often overlooked: if we don't *do* something, we're not going to *get* anything. We will get "what comes our way," which may or may not be what we want. Even if what we want occasionally *does* come our way, we almost always have to do *something* to partake of it. As the bumper sticker says: "Action for Satisfaction."

The second benefit is one of those "hidden values," like excitement hiding as fear, or caring hiding as hurt: the value of action is that *we make mistakes*. Mistakes show us what we need to learn.

"They're not going to talk about *mistakes* again, are they?" some readers may moan. Yes, we are. It may be a mistake to, but we are.

Many people read about the value of mistakes, say, "That makes sense," and then continue living their lives in the same avoid-mistakes-at-all-costs manner as before. They continue to play it safe, don't learn what they need to know, and then wonder why they're not closer to their Dream.

"Men stumble over the truth from time to time," Winston Churchill wrote, "but most pick themselves up and hurry off as if nothing happened." That is a mistake.

Mistakes show us what we need to learn. They indicate what we must study in order to have success. This "study" might be finding out more information, or it might mean more practice of what we already know. Either way, when we make a mistake, it's a golden arrow saying, "Study this if you want success."

"From error to error," Freud said, "one discovers the entire truth."

When people aren't ready to welcome mistakes as the great aids to education that they are, people deny them. Instead of *looking for* mistakes so that they can learn

The higher up you go,
the more mistakes
you're allowed.
Right at the top,
if you make enough of them,
it's considered to be your style.

FRED ASTAIRE

more and do better, people ignore, filter, and flat-out *deny* mistakes altogether.

This, of course, is another mistake.

All great people review their actions—even those actions that led to success—and ask themselves, "How could I have done this better." It's known as critical thinking. We *criticize* our behavior so that we can do *better* next time.

Most people, however, improperly use their critical ability—they use it to find reasons for why they should give up. "I did so many things *wrong*. Why should I bother trying? I quit."

Of course we're going to do things wrong. We should be grateful that we have the ability to recognize them. The mediocre never know what isn't quite right. They're satisfied with any old thing, and that's precisely what they wind up with.

You'll get a chance to do better next time. As long as you're actively involved in pursuing your goal, there will always be a next time. If you're moving toward your Dream, opportunity doesn't just knock once—it will knock you down.

The process of learning can be given in four steps:

1. Act.
2. Look for the mistakes (criticize).
3. Learn how to do it better next time.
4. Go to 1.

First we form habits,
then they form us.
Conquer your bad habits,
or they'll eventually
conquer you.

DR. ROB GILBERT

Let Go of Distractions

Distractions do not bring satisfaction. What are distractions? Anything not on the way to our goal that consumes our time, thoughts or emotional energy is a distraction.

There are the obvious distractions—the physical bad habits and addictions that people know are bad for them. There are the more subtle distractions—such as the habit of always focusing on the negative. (For lots more about this, and suggestions on how to overcome it, please read *You Can't Afford the Luxury of a Negative Thought.*) Then there are the distractions that *appear* to be wonderful things—virtues, even—but are distractions, nonetheless.

This latter category is the most tricky. These are actions that are indisputably good for you and/or are good for other people, but are *not* directly on the path to your goal. You could win a Nobel Prize for your charitable work, and, if your Dream were to be a pro golfer, all the charity work would, in fact, be a distraction.

Imagine that you are walking along a path. At the end of the path is your Dream. The way is clear, the goal is in sight. All you have to do is keep walking on your path till you reach your Dream.

Along the way, however, lining the path on either side, are distractions. It's their job to test you—to see if your goal is *really* the goal you want; to see if you are worthy of your Dream. The distractions can do *anything they want* to tempt you off your path: offer sex, food, fame, power, success in an area not part of your Dream, recognition, easy money—*anything*. What they *cannot* do is get *on* your path and *stop you*. Leaving the path is always *your choice*.

Choose to pursue your Dream. Follow your path.

*The sun will set
without thy assistance.*

THE TALMUD

Be Still, and Follow Your Dream

It is your job to fulfill your Dream.

It is *not* your job to right all the wrongs of the world, to teach everyone everything you know so that *they* will be able to right all the wrongs of the world, to in any way become involved with the struggle that always has been and probably always will be part of this planet, or anything else.

It is your job to fulfill your Dream.

If your Dream involves social or individual change, fine. Then saving *part* of the world is your business—but only part. If, for example, cleaner air is your passion, let someone else save the whales.

Trust that areas of your *concern*—but not of your Dream—*are* the Dreams of others. Let them fulfill their Dreams. You fulfill yours. "Nature arms each man with some faculty which enables him to do easily some feat impossible to any other," wrote Emerson. If we each bring our separate dish (our Dream) to the table of life—even if it's "just" dessert—we can all enjoy the banquet.

One great way of pursuing your Dream—and *only* your Dream—is keeping still. This begins by keeping still inside. We don't have to *react* to news or information that doesn't apply to our Dream. If we react to everything—including all the things other people think we should react to—we will have no mental or emotional energy left to focus on our Dream.

If it's not on our path, *it doesn't apply to us*. Someone just died somewhere in Russia. Does that *profoundly* sadden you? Why doesn't it? Because it doesn't much apply to your life. It's a tragedy for someone, but not for you. The same is true of all the other events and incidents delivered by the media and other gossipmongers. This "news" is designed to keep those *not* on their path in a state of constant distraction.

Maintain your inner stillness. Follow your Dream.

*Drawing on my fine command
of the English language,
I said nothing.*

ROBERT BENCHLEY

One way to obtain a greater inner silence is to maintain an outer silence. You need not have—or give—an opinion on every subject under the sun. "One of the lessons of history," wrote historian Will Durant, "is that nothing is often a good thing to do, and always a clever thing to say."

For those who prefer the scientific formula rather than the historical perspective, we present Albert Einstein: "If A is success in life, then A equals X plus Y plus Z. Work is X, Y is play and Z is keeping your mouth shut."

Even with something you *do* know about, something you have very definite opinions about, something you have every right to feel passionate about (we're talking about your Dream, of course), it's good to be quiet about that with others, too.

"It is a mistake for a sculptor or a painter to speak or write very often about his job," said Henry Moore. "It releases tension needed for his work." Keep the tension—the passion—within. Express it in deeds—in *actions*—not in words. Ben Franklin agreed with this, too: "Proclaim not all thou knowest, all thou owest, all thou hast, nor all thou can'st."

Of attainments, keep them to yourself. ("Be smart, but never show it," advised Louis B. Mayer.) Of problems, keep those to yourself as well. ("You can't tell your friend if you've been cuckolded." wrote Montaigne. "Even if he doesn't laugh at you, he may put the information to personal use.")

Be still. Pursue your dream. Follow your path.

*Opportunity is missed by most people
because it is dressed in overalls
and looks like work.*

THOMAS EDISON

*You can't build a reputation
on what you're GOING to do.*

HENRY FORD

Do the Work

You will achieve your Dream when you've done the necessary work. The good news is, you will achieve your Dream. The bad news is, there's work involved.

Pursuing your Dream requires work—mental, emotional and physical. Work is what we don't want to do, but we do anyway to get something else. To reach your Dream, you'll be called upon to do a lot of things you don't want to do.

Some people live in a fairy-tale fantasy about the attainment of their Dream. They think that every step on the way to their Dream should be effortless—a private jet picks them up on their front lawn and transports them to Paradise. Not only that, but they are *carried* to the private jet, and fed peeled grapes along the way.

That is a fantasy you had best dismiss. While you're at it, you might as well dismiss the fantasy that the work *ever* stops. Some people like to include a completely work-free life as part of their Dream. They tend to agree with Charlie McCarthy, who said, "Hard work never killed anybody, but why take the chance?" Alas, the work continues even *after* we have our Dream.

If we're still alive, there's still work to do.

The work may change form, but it remains as irksome as work always is. Actors work to find agent. Once an agent is found, they work to get a part. Once they get enough parts and are a star, they work to find the right script. The work never ends.

In other sections of the book, we've discussed the mental and emotional work involved. We would be remiss, however, if we didn't specifically mention *physical* work.

"It is a rough road that leads to the heights of greatness," Seneca said. Part of the roughness is doing all the mundane things you know you'll hire somebody *else* to do once you achieve your Dream. "Our main business is not to see what lies dimly in the distance," wrote Thomas

*The hand
is the cutting edge of the mind.*

JACOB BRONOWSKI

Carlyle, "but to do what lies clearly at hand." Is stuffing envelopes with your resume "at hand"? Stuff.

There are some things we can *never* hire anyone to do. If our Dream requires any personal physical ability or skill, for example, we have to work to maintain that. "Nothing I do can't be done by a ten-year-old—with fifteen years of practice," said magician Harry Blackstone, Jr. You can't hire someone to practice for you.

Sometimes we have an opportunity that requires extra work. Do it. "If an unusual necessity forces us onward, a surprising thing occurs," observed William James. "The fatigue gets worse up to a certain point, when, gradually or suddenly, it passes away and we are fresher than before!

"We have evidently tapped a new level of energy," James continues. "There may be layer after layer of this experience, a third and fourth 'wind.' We find amounts of ease and power that we never dreamed ourselves to own, sources of strength habitually not taxed, because habitually we never push through the obstruction of fatigue."

The French proverb sums it up: "One may go a long way after one is tired."

Some people say they would like "more luck." What they *usually* need is more *work*. "The harder you work," the saying goes, "the luckier you get." Luck itself is fairly evenly distributed. "Breaks balance out," said Darrell Royal. "The sun don't shine on the same ol' dog's ass every day."

A lot of people miss valuable opportunities—or flatly refuse to partake of them—due to their unwillingness to work. "Problems are only opportunities in work clothes," observed Henry J. Kaiser (sounding a lot like Edison).

Do the *necessary* work. A lot of people decide how much that is before they really *know* how much it will be. They say, "I've done enough work," and give up. They were wrong. It wasn't enough.

How do we know when it was enough? Simple. When we have what we want, it was enough. Until then, it

*I prefer Hostess fruit pies to
pop-up toaster tarts because
they don't require
as much cooking.*

CARRIE SNOW

wasn't. Do the work until it's enough—until you have your Dream.

It's a lot of *physical* work pursuing your Dream. Be prepared for it.

*If you want to win anything
—a race, your self, your life—
you have to go
a little berserk.*

GEORGE SHEEHAN

In Training for Success

Consider the pursuit of your dream a major athletic event. Train for it. What we do we become stronger in. That's true mentally, emotionally, and physically.

Physically. Keep fit. What keeps us fit? Exercise. A good diet. Precisely *what* constitutes a good diet, however, is so controversial, that we might open a special chamber of the Gap just to accommodate the many beliefs about nutrition. We can, nonetheless, offer with confidence this diet by Joel Weldon, found on the bulletin board of Dr. William Hellman:

BREAKFAST:

> **1/2 Grapefruit**
> **1 piece Whole Wheat Toast**
> **8 Oz. Skim Milk**

LUNCH:

> **4 Oz. Lean Breast of Chicken**
> **1 Cup Steamed Zucchini**
> **1 Oreo Cookie**
> **1 Cup Herb Tea**

MID-AFTERNOON SNACK:

> **Rest of Package of Oreo Cookies**
> **1 Quart Rocky Road Ice Cream**
> **1 Jar Hot Fudge**

DINNER:

> **2 Loaves Banana Bread**
> **1 Large Pepperoni Pizza**
> **1 Large Pitcher of Beer**
> **5 Milky Way Bars**
> **1 Entire Frozen Cheesecake—**
> **eaten directly from the freezer**

*My grandmother started
walking five miles a day
when she was sixty.
She's ninety-five now,
and we don't know
where the hell she is.*

ELLEN DEGENERIA

"I went on a diet," said Joe E. Lewis, "swore off drinking and heavy eating, and in fourteen days I lost two weeks."

"Only Irish coffee provides in a single glass all four essential food groups:" Alex Levine tells us, "alcohol, caffeine, sugar, and fat."

Emotions: Keep them flexible. We keep them flexible by practicing *unexpected* emotional reactions to life's challenges. For example, be loving even if you *don't* get your way. It won't cause people to come at you any less, but you will learn to be magnificent in the handling.

Mind: Keep it open. Eagerly consider new ideas, thoughts, suggestions, information, insights, perceptions and intuitions.

Comfort Zone: Keep expanding it. Each day, do at least *one* thing you don't want to do that has absolutely no practical benefit whatsoever. This keeps the comfort zone growing. For example, walking up and talking to people whom you *don't* want to meet will expand the comfort zone. Eventually, walking up and meeting strangers will be easy—comfortable. Then, when you see someone you *want* to meet, saying "Hello" will be an easy thing to do.

"Do something every day that you don't want to do." Mark Twain advised. "This is the golden rule for acquiring the habit of doing your duty without pain."

Your duty is fulfilling your Dream.

I am in earnest;
I will not equivocate;
I will not excuse;
I will not retreat a single inch;
and I will be heard.

WILLIAM LLOYD GARRISON

If It's Written in Stone, Bring Your Hammer and Chisel

Nothing is impossible. "The one unchangeable certainty," said John F. Kennedy, "is that nothing is unchangeable or certain." The more *improbable* something is, however, the more work it takes to achieve.

If there's something "impossible" about your Dream, do it anyway. "The greatest pleasure in life," says Walter Bagehot, "is doing what people say you cannot do." Benjamin Jowett adds, "Never retreat. Never explain. Get it done and let them howl."

Waiting around does not do it. *You* do it. "Things may come to those who wait," wrote Abraham Lincoln, "but only the things left by those who hustle." Thomas Edison (sounding a lot like Lincoln) said, "Everything comes to him who hustles while he waits."

Be bold. "Even God lends a hand to honest boldness," Menander wrote. "If you have an important point to make, don't try to be subtle or clever," Winston Churchill said. "Use a pile driver. Hit the point once. Then come back and hit it again. Then a third time—a tremendous whack."

For those who are concerned that their power might be too great, Sir Winston advises, "You will make all kinds of mistakes; but as long as you are generous and true, and also fierce, you cannot hurt the world or even seriously distress her."

Not only does boldness get us closer to what we want, it also has an important secondary benefit. "To know oneself," Camus wrote, "one should assert oneself."

How do we help guarantee success? Dorothea Brande suggested, "Act as if it were impossible to fail."

*They always say that
time changes things,
but you actually have to
change them yourself.*

ANDY WARHOL

If It's Written on the Wind, Bring Your Camera

Keep track of your successes—the achievement of the interim goals on the way to the Big One. Record them in some way.

At the end of each day, list all your accomplishments for that day. This is more than checking off what you did on various "to-do" lists. We usually accomplish far more than we set out to do. Listing *all* accomplishments at the end of the day—those planned, those spontaneous, and those serendipitous—gives a more complete picture of progress.

As this list grows, it becomes a testament to your power, your creativity, your achievement. Soon, the evidence becomes overwhelming: you *will* achieve your Dream. It's a logical outcome of the direction you are obviously heading.

It's also a good idea to *document* certain victories—with a camera, video, mementos, newspaper clippings, or paperwork. This helps show your direction and relative invincibility to others who may need persuading along the way.

Besides, in the years to come, your many biographers will appreciate whatever help you can give them.

*It is a good idea to obey all
the rules when you're young
just so you'll have the strength
to break them when you're old.*

MARK TWAIN

Shortcuts to Success

People, books, tapes, videos, magazines, etc. are all shortcuts to success. Learn from the accumulated wisdom of the ages. That's what it's been accumulating for.

A doctor, for example, is a shortcut to health. A teacher, a shortcut to learning. Any expert is a shortcut to success.

A picture may be worth 10,000 words, but a bit of advice from someone who has achieved a goal similar to yours, is worth 10,000 pictures.

With all advice, suggestions and guidance, we recommend the same thing: check it out for yourself. It may have worked for them, but it might not work for you.

Sometimes you learn how to do something by following advice. Other times, you learn to do precisely the *opposite* of what is recommended. Knowing a source of consistently *bad* advice is a godsend. Consult it regularly, then do the contrary. As the churchgoer once said, "Father, your sermons are like water to a drowning man."

When others give advice, they do you a favor. When you put that advice to good use, the favor is returned.

In the last analysis,
our only freedom
is the freedom
to discipline ourselves.

BERNARD BARUCH

Freedom Is Found in Discipline, Not Rebellion

When young, we are asked to follow rules that often lead us someplace we do not care to go. No wonder so many people learn to—in one way or another—rebel against rules.

In following *your* Dream, however, you will probably notice that you have more rules than ever before. What's going on? Isn't your Dream supposed to bring *freedom?*

Yes, and freedom is found in discipline. Discipline comes from the word *disciple*—being a devoted student. Think of discipline as a container. Once a container is constructed—and maintained—it can envelop your Dream.

A rule is a tool, as a drinking glass is a tool. Using the drinking glass, we can hold, carry and consume water. Yes, rules are restrictions, just as a drinking glass is a restriction. If we say, "I don't want any rules, because I don't want any restrictions," then we can also say, "I don't want any restrictions on my drinking glasses, either." An unrestricted drinking glass holds no water.

There are rules—*lots* of rules—to the things we use daily for fulfilling our Dream: walking, talking, reading, writing, and so many others. When we accept the rules of a given discipline and make them our own, we are no longer the disciple—we take a step toward mastery.

*If your parents
didn't have any children,
there is a good chance that
you won't have any.*

CLARENCE DAY

What Have You Learned?

No, this is not a book review, nor an essay exam—"Write a 10,000-word essay on 'What I have learned from this book.'" It's another one of those reviews of your entire life.

You've been fulfilling dreams for quite some time. They may have been your dreams, or they may have been the dreams of others. Either way, the *process* of dream fulfillment remains the same.

Review your list of accomplishments—the list you made about twenty years ago in the chapter *What Have You Accomplished?* For each achievement, ask yourself, "How did I do this? What did it take for me to fulfill that dream? What worked? What didn't?"

Begin to formulate your own set of "rules" on how *you* best achieve dreams. To fulfill our Dream, we need only examine our life, and do two things:

1. More of what works.

2. Less of what doesn't.

Leisure time is the five or six hours
when you sleep at night.

GEORGE ALLEN

INTERVIEWER: Your Holiness,
how many people work in the Vatican?
POPE JOHN XXIII: About half.

Nurture Yourself

It's important to nurture yourself while you're nurturing your Dream. In the large sense, of course, pursuing your dream *is* nurturing yourself. Along the way to your Dream, however, take time to be good to yourself.

Self-nurturing is not the same as self-indulgence. One of the most misused statements we've heard lately is, "I'm doing this to take care of myself." Usually, when people say this, they're running their old limitations under a new banner.

Succumbing to the comfort zone's demands is *not* "taking care of yourself."

Nurturing yourself means taking care of yourself *while you do what needs to be done*. This might mean working twenty hours on a project you *could* complete in fifteen. It does *not* mean not doing the project.

Learn to take the pressure off while you do what you do. When you think of *recreation,* think of re-creating your *attitude* toward the work at hand.

Rehabilitate your attitude toward words such as "work," "vacation" and "time off." The idea that we need "time off" comes from working for another to fulfill another's dreams. Now your life is directed toward fulfilling *your* Dream. Why would you want to take "time off" from that?

There are some activities on your path that are more enjoyable than others. Alternate these more pleasant activities with the more bothersome ones.

Learn to seek *satisfaction* in a job well done, rather than seek diversion in activities designed to distract you from the "harsh reality of work." That sort of diversion may be necessary for those who work for others. Remember, however: you're working for yourself now.

True nurturing is learning to enjoy the path, the process, the journey toward your Dream.

*Many of life's failures are
people who did not realize
how close they were to success
when they gave up.*

THOMAS EDISON

Persistence

Nothing succeeds like persistence. The common denominator of *all* successful people is their persistence.

"Nothing in the world can take the place of persistence," said Calvin Coolidge. "Talent will not; nothing is more common than unsuccessful men with talent. Genius will not; unrewarded genius is almost a proverb. Education alone will not; the world is full of educated derelicts. Persistence and determination alone are omnipotent."

Coolidge could be a role model for those who think one needs a sparkling personality to fulfill a Dream. "Silent Cal," as he was known, was so, well, *laid back,* that when told of his death, Dorothy Parker asked, "How could they tell?"

"Let me tell you the secret that has led to my goal," wrote Louis Pasteur. "My strength lies solely in my tenacity."

This same message rings throughout history—to win: persevere. The ancients knew it. "He who labors diligently need never despair;" wrote Menander, "for all things are accomplished by diligence and labor." "The drops of rain make a hole in the stone," said Lucretius, "not by violence, but by oft falling."

The same message is given from Goethe to Longfellow. Goethe: "Austere perseverance, harsh and continuous, may be employed by the least of us and rarely fails of its purpose, for its silent power grows irreversibly greater with time." Longfellow: "Perseverance is a great element of success. If you only knock long enough and loud enough at the gate, you are sure to wake up somebody."

Know what we've not had much of in this book? Poetry. Let's quote a persistence rhyme from Edmund Cooke:

> *You are beaten to earth?*
> *Well, well, what's that?*
> *Come up with a smiling face,*
> *It's nothing against you to fall down flat*
> *But to lie there—that's disgrace.*

Fall seven times,
stand up eight.

JAPANESE PROVERB

We will spare you what Napoleon, George Gobel, Churchill, Lincoln, Socrates, Orson Welles, Richard Nixon and the Lennon Sisters had to say about persistence. It's the same theme: "Keep going and you will win."

Persistence is a simple process:

1. What's the next step?
2. What's in the way of taking that step?
3. Remove* the obstacle.
4. Take the step.
5. Go to 1.

Without persistence, we may end up imitating Marlon Brando: "I coulda had class. I coulda been a contender. I coulda been somebody. Instead of a bum, which is what I am."

---

*In many cases, the word "Remove" can be replaced by "Disregard" or "Ignore."

*The real secret of success
is enthusiasm.*

WALTER CHRYSLER

Enthusiasm and Joy

Rather than comfort and joy, try enthusiasm and joy. Enthusiasm and joy are Siamese twins—it's hard to find one without the other.

Enthusiasm comes from the Latin *en theos*—one with the energy of the Divine. Here are some thoughts from Famous People, writing enthusiastically about enthusiasm.

"Nothing great was ever achieved without enthusiasm," wrote Emerson.

"I rate enthusiasm even above professional skill," said Sir Edward Appleton.

"Every production of genius," wrote Benjamin Disraeli, "must be the production of enthusiasm."

Joy is a feeling we can feel no matter what else is going on. The way to create joy is to do things joyfully. It's one of the easiest feelings to create. We need only remember to create it.

The Movie Hero's
Ten Commandments

1. *A man stands alone.*
2. *A man stands by his friends.*
3. *A man protects his family.*
4. *A man loves doing his work well.*
5. *A man is at home out of doors.*
6. *A man shares and plays fair.*
7. *A man speaks his mind.*
8. *A man hoards his smiles.*
9. *A man follows his dreams.*
10. *What he's got is what he is.*

RICHARD CORLISS

Horsing Around

To sum up the book thus far:

1. Find your horse.
2. Discover the direction the horse is going.
3. Ride the horse in that direction.

Happy trails!

When you get there,
there is no there there.
But there will be a pool.

DAVID ZUCKER

PART SIX

LIVING YOUR DREAMS

This section will make more sense when you've had a chance to live the first five sections for a while. In following the suggestions in those parts, you either have your Dream, or are well on the way to achieving it.

The question then arises, "What next?"

That's what this section is about. "There are two things to aim at in life: first, to get what you want; and after that, to enjoy it," wrote Logan Pearsall Smith.

"Only the wisest of mankind achieve the second."

*As Miss America,
my goal is to bring peace to
the entire world and then
to get my own apartment.*

JAY LENO

Choose New Goals

When your Dream is *almost* realized—but not quite—it's time to choose another goal.

The goal may remain the same, but the quantifying factors are raised. The goal to conduct an orchestra remains intact, for example, but the yearly salary increases from $100,000 to $200,000. Or, the goal may change entirely.

"Life affords no higher pleasure than that of surmounting difficulties," wrote Samuel Johnson, "passing from one step of success to another, forming new wishes and seeing them gratified."

When we realize one Dream, sometimes a deeper Dream reveals itself. At other times, a parallel Dream appears. The one that scares the hell out of you is probably it.

Just as the comfort zone knows no limits in keeping you from fulfilling your Dreams, it also has no limits on how large it can expand. It can grow infinitesimally small or infinitely large. It's your choice.

Our goals may change from one area of life to another, from Career/Professional, for example, to Social/Political—or any others. Or, they may stay in the same area.

In 1980, Sting said, "Given the choice of friendship or success, I'd probably choose success." He got it. In 1990, he chose again, "Friendship's much more important to me [now] than what I thought success was."

Celebrate your success. Now that you know that all this works, you can be *truly* bold. Reread the book from the beginning. It will make a lot more sense. Do the exercises. Choose another Dream.

Dream on.

*A man is rich in proportion to
the number of things which he
can afford to let alone.*

THOREAU

Wealth Is What You Can Live Without

This may seem like a strange chapter in a book about how to get *stuff,* but if you've listened for the underlying message, you'll know it fits right in.

When you tell most people, "Nothing outside yourself is going to make you happy; *you* must make yourself happy," they nod approvingly, and more often than not think, "I'll make myself happy when I have a new house, lover, job, meditation blanket, etc."

The shock that takes place when someone realizes, "I have my Dream and I'm still not totally happy," can be either depressing or enlightening. Depressing, if one thinks, "This was the *wrong dream.* Now I need to find the *right dream.—Then* I'll be happy." Enlightening, if someone says, "Maybe my happiness *does* depend on me," and begins the inward journey.

"Not the fruit of experience," wrote Walter Pater more than one hundred years ago, "but experience itself, is the end." Robert Townsend said it for our generation, "Getting there isn't half the fun—it's all the fun."

Elizabeth Taylor has a needlepoint pillow in her living room. It reads: "It's not the having, it's the getting."

What's the true value of setting a goal and achieving it? It's not obtaining the goal, but what we learn about *ourselves* along the way. To get to our Dream we must be focused, disciplined, persevering, caring, worthy, excited, enthusiastic, and passionate.

What do we learn about ourselves? How to be more focused, disciplined, persevering, caring, worthy, excited, enthusiastic, and passionate. Goals come and go, dreams fade, but these qualities travel with us wherever we go.

"There is no end. There is no beginning," said Federico Fellini. "There is only the infinite passion of life."

This is our true wealth—the riches we take with us, the joy we carry inside, the support we learned to give

There is only one success—
to be able to spend your life
in your own way.

CHRISTOPHER MORLEY

ourselves, and the self-loving that flows as a natural by-product of that support.

To the degree we can live without the things of this world, to that degree we are wealthy. The key word in that sentence is "live." We're not talking about austerity or sacrifice. We're talking about *living*. We *live* without them because, frankly, we can take them or leave them.

When we know how easy it is to fulfill a Dream (easy compared with how *impossible* most people believe it to be), we know we *can* take it. Once we are free to take it, we are free to leave it. "You never know what is enough," wrote Blake, "until you know what is more than enough."

Do not, however, make this an intellectual concept. Used as such, it's just another wonderful-sounding excuse for not pursuing your Dream. "The comfort zone hath power to assume a pleasing shape."

Go fulfill a few Dreams. *Know* you can do it. Have fun. *Then* decide for yourself.

Is this madness? Sure. "You have everything but one thing," Zorba the Greek told his young friend, "madness. A man needs a little madness or else—he never dares cut the rope and be free."

*Concerns for man and his fate
must always form
the chief interest of
all technical endeavors.
Never forget this in the midst
of your diagrams
and equations.*

ALBERT EINSTEIN

Give to Others of What You Know

On the way to your Dream, others helped you—others whom you couldn't possibly repay. The old saying comes to mind, "Don't repay a kindness; pass it on." Another saying comes to mind, "Others do not give to you; they really give to themselves."

After fulfilling a Dream or two (or twenty), we will be called upon to pass on some of what we have learned to others. This can be in many forms. Just as, "When the student is ready, the teacher appears," so, too, "When the teacher is ready, the student appears."

When it comes time to teach, teach from your *experience*. Go out and *do*, learn from the doing, then teach from the knowing. If you read a lot of books on the subject, memorize a lot of platitudes, and set yourself up as guru, that's not teaching; that's hiding.

When you know, others will know, and they will know to ask the right questions. And, as busy as you might be, you will stop and give them the right answers. Why? Their intention pulls it from you.

Also, you'll be an even nicer person.

"The common idea that success spoils people by making them vain, egotistic, and self-complacent is erroneous," wrote Somerset Maugham. "On the contrary, it makes them, for the most part, humble, tolerant and kind. Failure makes people bitter and cruel."

Cast not ye pearls before swine—but it's noble to pass on a few gems to properly eager pearl divers.

*There is more to life than
increasing its speed.*

GANDHI

The Tools for Achieving Material Goals Can Be Used for Achieving Non-Material Goals

The inner reflects the outer; the outer reflects the inner. What we learn from fulfilling Dreams in the outer world can be used for pursuing Dreams within ourselves.

After obtaining several material Dreams, you may wonder, "Where are these Dreams coming from?"

Important question. Seeking the answer to that question may begin an important inner quest.

"Try not to become a man of success," wrote Albert Einstein, "but rather try to become a man of value."

We're all in this alone.

LILY TOMLIN

The DO-IT Decade

As we mentioned at the start of this book, we refer to the last ten years of the 20th Century as *The DO-IT Decade*.

It's a significant period of time. It comes at the end of not just a century, but of a millennium. All the desires, aspirations, wishes, wants—Dreams, for short—that humans have had for the past thousand years can, in goodly measure, come true in the next ten.

It will take a lot of doers doing, however. That's our purpose in writing this book. We want people to know how to make Dreams come true—to become masters of manifestation.

When people give to themselves—when they fulfill their own Dreams—they are filled to overflowing. There are two interesting things about the overflow: (1) it is abundant, and (2) it can't be stored. What can one do with the overflow?

There's only one thing to do with it—give it away.

"Giving it away" is not standing on a street corner dispensing hugs. One gives of what one has. Whatever ability one has developed—in whatever area one has developed it—that's what is given.

Robert Ingersoll wrote at the end of the last century:

> *My creed is that:*
> *Happiness is the only good.*
> *The place to be happy is here.*
> *The time to be happy is now.*
> *The way to be happy is to make others so.*

And there we have one of the great open secrets of life: giving to others gives us more than we give away. When people discover this, there's no stopping them. The idea that doing for others is a reluctant duty—like paying taxes, or picking seeds out of a watermelon—vanishes.

Giving—like fear, guilt, unworthiness, and all the rest—was put here for our upliftment.

*We are here on earth
to do good to others.
What the others are here for,
I don't know.*

W. H. AUDEN

Doing for others feels good.

Don't take our word for it, however. Give it a go. See what you think. Go ahead.

DO IT!

Life is short. Live it up.

NIKITA KHRUSHCHEV

Humor and Fun

Life is a game. Like all games, it's only fun when we "take it all seriously"—when we get lost in the illusion, when it seems really *real*.

If someone stood over us while we were playing Monopoly, reminding us, "That's only paper; it's not real money. That's just plastic; those aren't real hotels. It's not a real jail they're going to send you to; it's just a square on a board," we'd throw him out of the room.

We want to believe the illusion is real, or else it wouldn't be any fun.

It wouldn't be any fun, either, if the competition wasn't very good and the score wasn't very close. Without that, it would be like playing tennis with a three-year-old. Lots of "victories," but very little fun.

"In terms of the game theory," explains George Leonard, "we might say the universe is so constituted as to maximize the play.

"The best games are not those in which all goes smoothly and steadily toward a certain conclusion, but those in which the outcome is always in doubt.

"Similarly, the geometry of life is designed to keep us at the point of maximum tension between certainty and uncertainty, order and chaos. Every important call is a close one. We survive and evolve by the skin of our teeth.

"We really wouldn't want it any other way."

Playing this game of life, something occasionally reminds us not to take it all too seriously. "Enjoy yourself," it says, "you'll never get out of this alive."

It's called humor.

"Humor is something that thrives between man's aspirations and his limitations," explained Victor Borge. "There is more logic in humor than in anything else. Because, you see, humor is truth."

He deserves Paradise
who makes his companions laugh.

THE KORAN

Among those whom I like or admire,
I can find no common denominator,
but among those whom I love,
I can: all of them make me laugh.

W.H. AUDEN

Alice-Leone Moats described Philadelphia society in this way: "The parties all reminded me of the Gay Nineties—all the men are gay and the women are in their nineties."

Humor is truth, truth is humor.

Humor is probably most refreshing when we use it to look at ourselves.

"You grow up," said Ethel Barrymore, "the day you have your first good laugh—at yourself." Friederich Nietzsche wrote: "One is healthy when one can laugh at the earnestness and zeal with which one has been hypnotized by any single detail in one's life." (What other book in the *world* would have Ethel Barrymore and Friederich Nietzsche agreeing on something within the same paragraph?)

When things are going awful, terrible, horrible—it helps to remember that, in six months, you'll be telling this "tragedy" as an anecdote. You'll have your friends laughing hysterically about it. If it'll be funny then, it's funny now. By remembering that in the middle of the chaos, you can take a deep breath and say to yourself, "Relax. This is funny."

"Humor is emotional chaos," James Thurber explained, "remembered in emotional tranquility."

"Humor is an affirmation of dignity," said Romain Gary, "a declaration of man's superiority to all that befalls him."

☆

And so we come to the end of *DO IT!* But not really. Come back often—review the tools of achieving Dreams.

"If I had more time," Blaise Pascal wrote, "I would write a shorter letter."

And if we had more time, we would have written a shorter book, but we didn't. But at least we DID IT.

We will close with this from Guillaume Apollinaire—

"Come to the edge," he said.
They said, "We are afraid."
"Come to the edge," he said.
They came.
He pushed them...
And they flew.

For Further Study:
Organizations Founded by
John-Roger

This is Peter, stepping out of my co-author character to tell you about some of the organizations founded by John-Roger.

J-R must like founding organizations. I certainly *hope* he likes founding organizations—he's founded enough of them. It's probably more accurate to say that organizations formed around John-Roger; he stands still for a while and teaches, and the people listening to him form organizations by which these teachings can be shared with others.

The organizations range from secular to the spiritual—that is, some are of The Gap, and some are not. I'll list them in approximate order of Gap-ness—starting with the purely secular.

Now that you've had a taste of J-R's teachings (through this book), you might like to explore some more. (In this book we have barely scratched the surface—he's been at it nonstop for the past 27 years.)

I'll be brief. You might want to ask your Master Teacher which, if any, of these you might like to pursue.

The Heartfelt Foundation is dedicated to service. They do various community projects, large and small, all over the world. If you'd like to take part—or organize a service project in your community—give them a call. 2101 Wilshire Blvd., Santa Monica, CA 90403; 213-828-0535.

Institute for Individual and World Peace. Just as it says. If you want to learn more about peace and how you can effect it—or if you have any ideas to contribute—drop them a line. 2101 Wilshire Blvd., Santa Monica, CA 90403; 213-828-0535.

University of Santa Monica. Offers an M.A. in Applied Psychology, including the Awakening the Inner Counselor program. Approved by the State of California. Write or call for a brochure. 2107 Wilshire Blvd., Santa Monica, CA 90403; 213-829-7402.

(Those organizations that would be classified as Gap-like begin here.)

Movement for Spiritual Inner Awareness (MSIA) is for those who want to live in a way that makes spirit and God a part of their lives. MSIA has no formal membership, dues, rules or dogma. It encourages people in their own experience of the divine, without restricting personal choices. The booklet "About MSIA" describes MSIA and its goals. You can also find out if J-R's TV show "That Which Is" is available in your area. Write or call MSIA, Box 3935, Los Angeles, CA 90051; 213-737-4055.

Discourses. John-Roger's Soul Awareness Discourses are the most complete, effective and delightful course in Spirit I know. You simply read one a month at your own pace. Each Discourse contains about 30 pages of text and more than 60 blank pages for your own daily notes, reminders, dreams, discoveries, affirmations or anything else you'd like. They're $100 per year (12 Discourses), and I can't recommend them too highly. For more information, please contact MSIA.

Mandeville Press. Publishes J-R's earlier books, including *Relationships—The Art of Making Life Work, The Power Within You,* and *Wealth and Higher Consciousness.* On a more spiritual note, there's *Loving...Each Day, The Spiritual Promise, The Spiritual Family* and *The Way Out Book.* Other books are available. They also publish *The New Day Herald,* a bimonthly newspaper of articles on, mostly, loving. A vast collection of John-Roger on audio and video tapes is available, looking at life from a spiritual yet practical point of view. A free catalog is available from MSIA.

Other Books (and Stuff) Published by Prelude Press

This is still Peter. I thought I'd tell you about some of the books published by Prelude Press. This may seem like a shameless commercial. It is not. As author (or co-author) and publisher of these books, I say it's not a commercial—it is an exercise in blatant egoism.

DO IT! Audio Tapes

Read by Academy Award nominee Sally Kirkland, Christopher McMullen and yours truly. Complete and unabridged, six cassettes, $22.95.

LIFE 101:
Everything We Wish We Had Learned About Life in School—But Didn't

The overview book of the *LIFE 101 Series*. The idea behind *LIFE 101* is that everything in life is for our upliftment, learning and growth—including (and, perhaps, especially) the "bad" stuff. "The title jolly well says it all," said the *Los Angeles Times*—jolly well saying it all. 400 pages. **Trade paperback,** $9.95. **Audio Tapes** (complete and unabridged, five cassettes), $19.95. **Wristwatch** (Paul LeBus designed), $35.00.

You Can't Afford the Luxury of a Negative Thought

This is the first book John-Roger and I co-authored. In its 622 pages, we've done all that we can to make a "serious" subject (life-threatening illness) light. As we point out in the introduction, "This is not just a book for people with life-threatening illnesses. It's a book for anyone afflicted with one of the primary diseases of our time: negative thinking." **Trade paperback,** $14.95. **Audio Tapes** (complete and unabridged, eight cassettes), $22.95. **Wristwatch,** $35.00.

Focus on the Positive:
The You Can't Afford the Luxury of a Negative Thought Workbook

Specific exercises to help you eliminate the negative and latch on to the affirmative. 200 pages. **Trade paperback,** $11.95.

How to Survive the Loss of a Love

This is an entirely new edition, completely revised and updated. 212 pages. **Hardcover,** $10.00. **Audio Tapes** (complete and unabridged, two cassettes), $11.95.

To achieve your goal,
your life may sound
like a perfume counter—
full of Passion and Obsession,
leading to Joy.

Index

A

Abilities, 11, 13, 27, 47, 221, 247, 249, 251, 269, 363
Ability Suit, 125, 255, 305
Ability Suit Practice Area, 125, 255, 305
Accomplishments, 211, 215, 433
Achievement, 9, 315, 317, 331
Acting, 137
Action, 5, 25, 39, 87, 89, 91, 93, 107, 141, 143, 147, 223, 225, 281, 411, 413
Activity, 167, 169
Adams, Philip, 401
Ade, George, 40
Adolescence, 5
Adults, 105, 125
Advice, 19, 126
Affirmations, 301
African Bushman, 50
Agreements, 279, 285
AIDS, 107
Alda, Alan, 28
Alinsky, Saul, 53
Allen, Dennis, 62
Allen, Fred, 183, 237, 336
Allen, George, 440
Allen, Gracie, 148
Allen, Woody, 51, 53, 64, 202, 244
Alpha Centauri, 373

Alphabet, 25, 29
Alternative, 125
Altman, Robert, 194
Amboy Dukes, 297
Amory, Cleveland, 339
Anderson, Margaret, 201
Anglicanism, 193
Anger, 5, 25, 29, 31, 47, 49, 63, 65, 79, 81, 87, 99, 101, 115, 129, 131, 331, 379
ANI-HU, 351
Apollinaire, Guillaume, 471
Appleton, Larry, 307
Appleton, Sir Edward, 447
Aquarium, 15
Aristotle, 33, 371
Armstrong, Louis, 6
Asimov, Isaac, 107
Aspirations, 71
Astaire, Fred, 412
Asylum, 121
Attitudes, 79, 103
Auberjonis, Rene, 373
Auden, W. H., 205, 464, 468
Augsburger, David, 130
AUM(OHM), 349
Aurelius, Marcus, 100, 388
Avila, St. Theresa of, 247
Awareness, 131

B

Bach, Richard, 144, 181
Bacon, Francis, 32
Baez, Joan, 186

Bagehot, Walter, 431
Baldwin, James, 183
Barr, Roseanne, 181
Barry, Dave, 55
Barrymore, Ethel, 469
Bartoukomous, Balki, 307
Baruch, Bernard, 436
Bass, 353
Baths, 337
Beaton, Sir Cecil, 401
Beckett, Samuel, 12
Bedazzled, 259
Beecham, Sir Thomas, 406
Beelzebub, 49
Beliefs, 41, 43, 87, 89, 91, 99, 105, 115, 303
Bellamy, Guy, 107
Benchley, Robert, 398, 418
Benny, Jack, 403
Berlin, Irving, 307
Berra, Yogi, 250
Beverly Hillbillies, The, 254
Bible, 19
Big Dream, 9, 227
Bishop, Russell, 57, 70
Bixby, Lawrence, 492
Blackstone Jr., Harry, 423
Blake, William, 368, 457
Blame, 387
Blanton, Dr. Smiley, 222
Body, 103
Boldness, 286
Bonaparte, Napoleon, 280
Book of the Dead, The, 38
Boorstin, Daniel J., 404
Borge, Victor, 467
Boulanger, Nadia, 328
Bovee, 266
Brande, Dorothea, 431

Brando, Marlon, 445
Braun, Wernher von, 181
Breath, 349, 351
Breathing, 335
Breathing Meditation, 349
Brecht, Bertolt, 66
Brenan, Gerald, 373
Bronowski, Jacob, 422
Brooks, Mel, 38, 65
Brown, A. Whitney, 55
Brown, Norman O., 199
Browning, Robert, 65
Bryan, William Jennings, 51
Buatta, Mario, 212
Buchan, John, 191
Burdon, Eric, 324
Burke, Edmund, 189, 380
Burns, George, 218
Burroughs, William S., 405
But, 9, 17, 19
Butkus, Dick, 55

C

Cage, John, 164, 272
Campbell, Joseph, 151
Camus, 431
Candle, 353
Capote, Truman, 238
Career, 135
Career/Professional, 167, 169, 180 - 187, 251, 253
Caring, 99
Carlyle, Thomas, 352, 423
Carmel, California, 15
Carson, Johnny, 65
Catholicism, 193
Cats, 185
Center, the, 349
Chafee Jr., Zechariah, 409

Davy, Sir Humphrey, 373
Day, Clarence, 438
De Fènelon, François, 48
De Vries, Peter, 55, 205
Deadline, 103
Death, 65, 103 - 105, 107
DECIDAMP, 347
Degeneria, Ellen, 428
Dependent, 5
Depression, 47
Devil, 39
Diaghelev, 183
Dickens, Charles, 376
Dickson, R. A., 74
Disappointment, 47
Discipline, 437
Discomfort, 37, 65
Discouragement, 27, 31,
49, 67, 109, 111, 113, 115,
129, 131
Disraeli, Benjamin, 53, 447
Distractions, 415
DO IT Decade, The, 9, 463
Double Entendre, 321
Douglas, Norman, 276
Downs, Hugh, 51
Dreams, 286, 353
Durant, Will, 419
Dylan, Bob, 68, 206, 232

E

E, 353
E.A.R., 347
Easter Bunny, 5
Edison, Thomas A., 20,
420, 431, 442
Egypt, 191
Eiffel Tower, 7

Einstein, Albert, 72, 105,
146, 419, 458, 461, 494
Eisenhower, Dwight D.,
307
Ekland, Britt, 179
Elephant, 49
Elimination, 319
Eliot, T. S., 185
Ellis, Dr. Albert, 389
Emerson, Ralph Waldo, 10,
118, 188, 239, 403, 417,
447
Emotions, 33, 63, 79, 129,
131, 293, 351, 379, 429
Empathy, 351
En Theos, 293, 447
Encouragement, 109, 111,
113, 115, 131
Energy, 7, 27, 43, 79, 81,
83, 85, 87, 99, 101, 111,
115, 129, 215, 273, 315,
317, 323, 325, 327, 331,
341, 359
English, 25
Enough, 161
Enthusiasm, 446 - 447
Entryway, 123
Environment, 35
Ewing, J. R., 190
Excitement, 7, 27, 29, 131
Exercise, 335
Expansion, 375, 377
Expectations, 33
Experience, 35, 41
Expression, 323

F

Failure, 41, 49, 77, 113,
117, 403

Fame, 237 - 239
Family, 213
Faulkner, William, 396
Fear, 5, 7, 25, 27, 29, 31, 33, 35, 37, 49, 59, 61, 63, 65, 79, 81, 83, 85, 101, 111, 129, 131, 229, 331, 379, 381
Feelings, 5
Fellini, Federico, 455
Fight or Flight Response, 63, 65
Fitzgerald, F. Scott, 9
Flame Meditation, 353
Forbes, Malcolm, 183
Ford, Henry, 27, 124, 420
Forgiveness, 131
Fosdick, Harry Emerson, 216
Fowler, Gene, 396
France, 7
Franklin, Benjamin, 151, 182, 403, 419
Freedom, 409, 437
Freud, Sigmund, 411
Friedman, Bruce Jay, 198
Friends, 129, 221
Fritz, Robert, 150
Frost, Robert, 187
Fry, Christopher, 369
Fulfillment, 3, 9, 43, 47, 157, 159, 241
Fuller, Margaret, 240
Fun, 467
Fun/Recreation, 197
Future, 13, 119

G

Gabor, Zsa Zsa, 175
Galbraith, John Kenneth, 21
Gandhi, 460
Gap, The, 193
Garland, Judy, 309
Garrison, William Lloyd, 430
Gary, Romain, 469
Genius, 286
Gershwin, George, 307
Gide, André, 142
Gielgud, Sir John, 307
Gilbert, Dr. Rob, 82, 296, 414
Gilbert, W.S., 42
Gillis, Dobie, 180
Giving, 175, 463
Glamour, 233
Global, 9
Goal-fulfillment mechanism, 137, 139, 275
Goal-setting mechanism, 137, 139
Goals, 81, 135, 137, 139, 159, 163, 167, 169, 217, 223, 289, 313
God, 43, 71, 95, 97, 103, 143, 175, 192 - 193, 195, 204, 215, 221, 241, 253, 323, 347, 349, 397, 431
Goethe, 203, 286, 443
Golden Girls, The, 390
Goldwyn, Samuel, 52
Good Earth, The, 349
Gould, Tim, 53

I

If Only, 17
Ignorance, 35
Imagination, 117, 119, 121, 161, 297
Impatience, 267
Inaction, 37, 49
Independent, 5
Information Retrieval System, 123, 255, 305
Ingersoll, Robert, 463
Inner classroom, 121
Inner retreat, 121
Inner work, 125
Inner Worlds of Meditation, 347
Insight Consulting Group, 395
Intellectual, 93
Intention, 147, 149, 151
International House of Pancakes, 300
Isaiah, 80

J

Jackson, Glenda, 96
James, William, 191, 245, 304, 388, 423
Jeopardy, 29, 223
Jesus, 19, 195
Job, 241
John-Roger, 347, 361
Johnson, Samuel, 53, 453
Jonathan Joffrey Crab, 291
Jones, Shirley, 308
Jong, Erica, 126
Jordan, Barbara, 191

Jowett, Benjamin, 431
Joy, 173, 447
Jung, C. G., 174

K

Kaiser, Henry J., 423
Kaufman, Margo, 76
Keillor, Garrison, 54
Keller, Helen, 214, 344
Kempton, Sally, 22
Kennedy, Jacqueline, 308
Kennedy, John F., 102, 401, 431
Kennedy, Rose, 235
Kerr, Jean, 233
Kesey, Ken, 270
Khrushchev, Nikita, 466
King, Basil, 362
Kingsley, Charles, 26
Kissinger, Henry A., 189, 392
Kline, Kevin, 307
Knowledge, 93
Koestler, Arthur, 316
Koran, 468

L

Laing, R. D., 262
Larson, Gary, 55
Later, 327, 367, 369
Lawrence, D. H., 173
Lawyer, 94 - 95
Laziness, 366 - 367
Leach, Reggie, 340
Leadership, 189
Learning, 7, 85
Lebowitz, Fran, 110
LeCarre, John, 53

Lee, Gypsy Rose, 398, 407
Leno, Jay, 452
Leonard, George, 467
Leonard, Joseph, 149
Lessons, 121
Levine, Alex, 429
Lewis, Jerry, 288
Lewis, Joe E., 429
Lie, 165
Life, 131, 217
LIFE 101, 11, 183, 193
LIFE 101 Series, The, 11
Light, 123, 127, 349
Limitations, 19, 39, 71, 79,
85, 121, 247, 249, 251,
267, 269, 301, 331
Lincoln, Abraham, 43, 45,
294, 431
Little Shop of Horrors,
395
Lodge Jr., Henry Cabot,
307
Lois, George, 314
Longfellow, Henry
   Wadsworth, 168, 443
Longfellow, Layne, 30
Los Angeles, CA, 23, 347
Losing, 231
Love, 99, 152 - 153, 173,
175, 177 - 178, 201, 203,
349
Luce, Clare Boothe, 191
Lucretius, 35, 443
Luther, Martin, 398
Lyon, Bill, 55

M

MacArthur, General
   Douglas, 252

Madness, 37
Madonna, 132, 253
Magic, 286
Main Room, 123
Maintenance, 251, 263
Maltz, Maxwell, 279, 403
Mame, Auntie, 403
*Man From U.N.C.L.E.,
   The,* 180
Mandeville Press, 347, 361
Mann, Horace, 279
Mansfield, Katherine, 215
Maritain, Jacques, 199
Marquis, Don, 258
Marriage, 172, 205, 235,
278
Marriage/Family, 167, 169,
173, 175, 177 - 179, 185,
201, 251, 253
Marx, Groucho, 64
*Mary Tyler Moore Show,
   The,* 310
Maslow, Abraham, 264
Massage, 337
Master Creator, i
Master of your Universe,
125
Master Teacher, 125, 143,
247, 249, 255, 257, 265,
269, 305
Matthew, Book of, 19
Maugham, Somerset, 459
Mayer, Louis B., 419
McCarthy, Charlie, 421
McGinley, Phyllis, 195
McWilliams, Peter, 389
Mead, Margaret, 371
Meditation, 125, 347, 349,
351, 353, 355, 357
Menander, 443

Rosten, Leo, 384
Rothschild, Sir Nathan
   Meyer, 334
Rousseau, Jean-Jacques,
400
Rowe, Nicholas, 382
Royal, Darrell, 423
Rubin, Bob, 53
Rudner, Rita, 175, 278
Ruskin, John, 120
Russell, Bertrand, 34, 185

S

Sacred Room, 125, 255
Sanctuary, 119, 121, 123,
125, 143, 145, 245, 247,
255, 301, 305, 309
Santa Claus, 4 - 5
Sarnoff, David, 185
Sartre, Jean-Paul, 173
Satisfaction, 319
School, 211
Schopenhauer, Arthur, 156
Schuller, Dr. Robert, 245
*Scottish Himalayan
   Expedition, The,* 286
Screenplay, 9
Seeding, 359
Self, 159
Self esteem, 61
Selfing, 157
Selfish, 157, 171
Seneca, 421
Sensitivity, 17
Sex, 199, 201, 320 - 321
Sexual, 319
Shakes, Ronnie, 310
Shakespeare, William, 33,
37, 114, 154, 235

Shaw, George Bernard,
116, 159, 162, 170, 246,
309, 338
Sheehan, George, 426
Shelley, Mary
   Wollstonecraft, 140
Shortcuts, 435
Silbar, Jeff, 306
Silence, 350, 352, 356
Singer, Isaac Bashevis, 330
Skinner, B.F., 89
Smith, Alexander, 152
Smith, Logan Pearsall, 51,
451
Smith, Margaret, 86
Smith, W. Eugene, 342
Snead, Sam, 307
SO-HAWNG, 351
Social/Political, 167, 169,
189, 191, 213, 251, 253
Socrates, 178
Solzhenitsyn, Alexander, 63
Sophocles, 35
Soprano, 355
Specific, 343
Spielberg, Steven, 201
St. Vincent Millay, Edna,
55
Star-Trek, 123
Stein, Gertrude, 244
Steinberg, David, 39
Steinem, Gloria, 24
Sting, 290, 453
Stomach, 33, 39, 43, 47
Stretching, 335
Streisand, Barbara, 343
Success, iv, 18, 41, 77, 183,
227, 229, 340, 435, 456
Success Mechanism, 329
Suppression, 323

Sylvania's Halo of Light
  Television, 125

T

Talmud, 416
Tate, Jessica, 308
Taylor, Elizabeth, 455
Teacher, 125
Teaching, 459
Television, 15, 23, 25, 61
Temple, Shirley, 4
Tenor, 355
Tension, 331, 333, 335
Teresa, Mother, 239
Thatcher, Margaret, 360
THO, 351
Thomson, Virgil, 407
Thoreau, Henry David, iv,
32, 364, 454
Thoughts, 5, 25, 35
Thurber, James, 408, 469
Tim, Tiny, 249, 312
Time, 163, 167, 243,
260 - 261
Tithing, 359
Tomlin, Lily, 183, 256, 462
Tones, 349
Tools, 79
Tooth Fairy, 5, 299
Toscanini, Arturo, 307
Touch, 337
Townsend, Robert, 189, 455
Toys, 125
Traditional, 125
Trauma, 57
Treasure Map, 303
Trillin, Calvin, 53, 175
Trine, Ralph Waldo, 157
Trolls, 289, 291

True Self, 157
Truman, Harry, 191
Truth, 13, 17, 19, 223
Try, 16 - 17
Turner, Lana, 183
Turner, Tina, 307
Twain, Mark, 98, 149,
294 - 295, 305, 354, 367,
434

U

Uncomfortable, 5, 7, 25,
27, 29, 51, 67, 71, 275,
277, 377
Unity, 351
Unlimitedness, 121
Unworthiness, 5, 25, 29,
31, 41, 43, 45, 49, 61, 65,
79, 81, 95, 97, 101, 129,
131, 325, 329, 331, 379
Up the Organization, 189
Updike, John, 189, 326
Uplifting, 13
Utopia, 187

V

Vaughan, Bill, 235
Vidal, Gore, 191, 201
Video Screen, 123, 255, 305
Vision, 9
VISTA, 241
Visualization, 119, 121,
297, 347

W

Waiting For Godot, 12
Waitley, Denis, 226, 378

*Each handicap is like a
hurdle in a steeplechase,
and when you ride up to it,
if you throw your heart over,
the horse will go along, too.*

LAWRENCE BIXBY

*If you would like to receive
information about future
books, tapes, lectures, etc.
by John-Roger and
Peter McWilliams,
please send
your name and address
to:*

*Prelude Press
8159 Santa Monica Boulevard
Los Angeles, California
90046*

Thank you.

Imagination is more important than knowledge.

ALBERT EINSTEIN

About the Authors

JOHN-ROGER, an educator, has been very busy during the past twenty-seven years. He has traveled the world, teaching, lecturing, writing and presenting seminars on just about every conceivable area of personal growth. He founded several organizations dedicated to a broad range of projects including health, education, spirit, philosophy, service, integrity, corporate excellence and individual and world peace. He has written twenty-five books, recorded hundreds of audio and video tapes, and has a nationally syndicated television show, *That Which Is*.

PETER McWILLIAMS published his first book, a collection of poetry, at the age of seventeen. His series of poetry books went on to sell more than 3,000,000 copies. A book he co-authored on meditation was #1 on the *New York Times* best-seller list. He is the co-author of *How to Survive the Loss of a Love*. His *The Personal Computer Book* was a best-seller. He is a nationally syndicated columnist, teaches seminars, and has appeared on the *Oprah Winfrey Show*, *Donahue*, *Larry King* and *The Today Show*.

Here I am
at the end of the road,
at the top of the heap.

POPE JOHN XXIII